THE WEAVER

THE
WEAVER

by

Harold E. Dye

BROADMAN PRESS
Nashville, Tennessee

4252-30

ISBN: 0-8054-5230-3

Library of Congress catalog card number: 52-10101
Dewey Decimal Classification Number: 240

CONTENTS

CONTENTS

I

The Navajo Rug

I TURNED the ugly snout of the jeep from the canyon road and bounced it over the mesquite clumps toward the cluster of brown adobe houses with their lazily turning windmills. The *hacienda* looked just as it did during my vacation two years before. It looked, in fact, exactly as it did when redoubtable old Don de Villegas y Flores flung it across the path of marauding Apaches a century and a half ago. Adobe houses are indigenous; they are ageless as the sands upon which they are built.

"Hola, caballero!"

There was a faint swishing sound, and my arms were jerked from the steering wheel and pinioned by a snaky loop which tautened like a band of steel. I kicked at the brake in a reflex action that brought the jeep to a skidding stop while the motor raced on in neutral. My knee had caught the gear-shift lever.

"Let me loose—you—locoed imitation of Pancho

Villa's stepson! And don't call me a horse!" I yelled
back as I loosened the rope and switched off the igni-
tion.

A huge straw *sombrero* sailed toward me from the
other end of the rope.

"Ho, ho! The gringo she steel do not know the Spanish. I deed not call you a horse. A horse, she ees a *caballo*. A *caballero*, she ees a gentleman. I deed not call
you a horse, but all the same you act like some horses
I have."

"Same old Pablo," I grinned, "always ready to
argue."

"*Como te vas?*" A giggling mass detached itself from
the shade of the sprawling adobe and waddled toward
me. Pablo was brushed aside. I saw huge arms spread
wide as I jumped down from the jeep.

"*Tia* Margarita! You get prettier all the time."
I managed to duck under her widespread arms to
aim a kick at my young friend Pablo. My arms burned
where his lasso had bitten into them. With a boyish
laugh the Mexican *vaquero* darted for protection behind the voluminous skirts of his aunt. She beamed at
me.

"You are, *señor, mucho* careless weeth the truth. I
like to hear such lies, though. *Yo creo*—that is, I believe
—that I am just *muchachita*, after all."

She did not look much like a "little girl," I reflected.
I was pretty sure that she could throw a horseshoe a

hundred yards with her muscular arm. But I also knew that if light-heartedness and affection be qualities of girlhood, *Tia* Margarita could qualify easily. She was known to every passing cowboy as *Tia*—Aunt—Margarita.

"Come eento the house," she invited. "I have the grease hot for the *tortilla* and we weel have mucho *enchiladas*. Pablo," she whirled toward the youth who was looking at me with grinning watchfulness, *"andale con raices de mesquite! Pronto!"*

"I better get the mesquite roots queek or she weel knock me on the *cabeza* weeth one," laughed Pablo as he darted past my swinging foot. He knew that I was watching for my chance to avenge my loss of dignity.

I crossed over to the jeep and lifted out my duffel bag.

"Hey!" shouted Pablo, who was there before me. "Thees jeep she have the caboose like a train!" He pointed to the stock trailer which I had towed into the desert.

"You are right, *mi enemigo*; that is a caboose for the *caballeros*. We are going to haul them to where we have to ride them."

"Why cannot you learn to speak the Spanish?" howled my dark-skinned friend. "I speak the Eenglish perfectly, and I am not so very much smarter than you. I do not go calling a horse a gentleman, or the gentleman I do not call the horse. *Y por favor* I am not going to ride the *caballero*. You do not ride a gentleman."

"Pablo!" came a shriek from the doorway, "*andale pronto o te mato!*"

"I understand that," I said. "She called you a tomato."

Pablo stood with his hands on his hips. He was puffing slightly. I noticed that he had grown a jaunty little mustache since I had seen him last. It gave him even a more quizzical look, and he was already just an animated question mark. He lifted his arms and shrugged expressively. "She no call me a tomato," he said weakly. "She say she weel keel me." He made for the pile of mesquite roots by the corral corner.

The flickering oil lamp cast huge, misshapen shadows on the white-washed walls as *Tia* Margarita moved about the oilcloth-covered table serving up hot, sizzling *enchiladas*. These delicious concoctions are made by frying corn *tortillas* (thin pancakes) covered with grated cheese and chili sauce, stacking them three deep on a plate, and topping the whole with a fried egg and shreds of lettuce. *Frijoles* (pinto beans), fried and mashed, garnished with *fritos* (corn wafers), and Spanish rice were side dishes. Strong coffee, poured from the hissing spout of a granite-blue pot, helped wash away the sting of the doubly hot *enchiladas*.

"So you are come to hunt the Indians, *que no?*" asked my sweating hostess as she leaned over to refill my cup.

"Not just exactly," I replied. "What I am really looking for is a certain kind of Navajo rug, as I explained in my letter to Pablo."

"But you have to hunt the Indians so you can get the rug," persisted my logical waitress. "Suppose the Indians, they do not like for you to stick long nose into their business?" she snickered.

"Then *mi amigo* gets the long nose sliced off weeth the Navajo hunting knife," came the muffled observation of Pablo, whose mouth was full of *tortilla*.

"I'll have to take my chance on that. I never was too crazy about the looks of my nose, but I do prefer to have it attached to my face. Anyway, that is just why I am taking you along, Pablo. You can be my bodyguard."

"Eef Pablo she guard any body, eet weel be thees one." He tapped his chest. "And eef thees Navajo she wave the *cuchilla* een the air, thees Pablo she run like Gila monster after grasshopper."

"*Sin duda,*" murmured *Tia* Margarita.

"She says 'weethout doubt,'" translated Pablo, grinning at me. "She love me *mucho*."

"Tell me more of thees rug of the Navajos. And why do you want eet so much?" insisted *Tia* Margarita as I waved the coffeepot aside.

"A long time ago," I related, "there lived in the San-
gre de Cristo mountains of northern New Mexico a
mysterious race of human beings known as the Gallinas
people. Traces of their dwelling places are found in
the Gallinas Canyon near Las Vegas, as are mysterious
towers of stone built by them for some unknown purpose. These people completely disappeared from the
earth. Whether they died of disease or were massacred
by unfriendly Indian tribes is not known. Certain
petrographs, or rock paintings, have been found in a
cave. Recently it was discovered that a certain Navajo
Indian woman was weaving the same symbols in her
rugs. That woman lives in Arizona, up near the New
Mexico border. An eastern university has asked me
to find her and get a sample of her weaving which contains these symbols. Archeologists—these are men who
study the evidences left by ancient peoples," I explained to my unlearned companions, "are interested
in trying to discover whether there can be any possible
connection between that surviving Navajo woman and
the vanished Gallinas people."

Tia Margarita had sat down across the table from
me. She rested her double chin on her brown hands
and gazed at me with black eyes sparkling with interest.
I felt her breathless attention.

"You theenk thees Navajo woman who weaves the
fonny rugs may be come from these 'chicken' peoples?"

"I don't know. The men of science will have to figure that out—if they can. My work will be finished as soon as I get the rug and deliver it to them. I was glad to get the assignment and to get to come back to Arizona," I added. "I shall never forget the trip which Pablo and I made in search of the night-blooming cereus two years ago. He is a little *loco* in the *cabeza*," I grinned at my Spanish-American friend and caught the glint of merriment in his own eye, "but I like him. Besides, he can make good coffee."

And so it was that Pablo and I set forth at daybreak with two rangy little mustangs in the jeep trailer, on our way to Navajo land in the search of the ghosts of forgotten peoples. I do not know to this day whether or not my ultimate delivery of a beautiful Navajo rug shook the scientific world of the anthropologists, the archeologists, and the paleontologists; I do not know whether or not some brilliant antiquarian is now engaged in writing a book explaining the mystery of the shadowy Gallinas people. I only know that I found a treasure, rich in the imperishable lore of living, and I set down here the story of Bi-mah Begay and her wonderful rug and what that rug told me of a richer tapestry, the age-old tapestry of life. I found a blueprint for the citadel of the human soul—drawn by the hand of God.

II

God and the Weaver

BATTLESHIP ROCK drifted through the shimmering desert mirage like a ghostly Spanish galleon on a sea of dreams. From her topmost point a lone cloud fluttered like a pirate's pennant. As though flung from the storm-tossed hold of the ship, somnolent sheep rode the illusory waves which the mirage spilled over the sandhills. A Navajo herder, his gay head-scarf flaming, walked on the simulated water, the yelps of his mangy dog bouncing from the sails of the stone ship, and rattling impotently down her rock-sheathed sides.

Far beyond, and toward the east where the horizon bent toward infinity, the mountains of southern Colorado sawed at the turquoise sky fourteen thousand feet above sea level. Here the world stretched on forever. And here there was peace—ineffable peace.

We waved at the distant sheepherder. Pablo yelled, *"Hola, amigo!"* The Indian looked briefly our way

and shied a stone at a wandering old ewe that dreamed
of greener pastures somewhere beyond the blue hills.
My horse snorted as the dog bounded our way through
the clumps of blue sage.

"That Eendeyon, she ees not civilized," grumbled
Pablo when the sheepherder failed to return our salute.

Our trail, a bare, brown streak through the aromatic
sage, led around the northernmost tip of Battleship
Rock. Now and then it bent to avoid the outthrust
arm of a shaggy, needle-upholstered cholla cactus which
stood innocently until a horseman came abreast and
then slapped him on the thigh with impish glee. If that
thigh did not at the moment happen to be covered by
leather *chaparejos*, certain writhing gymnastics inevita-
bly proclaimed that the horseman had been awakened
from his dreaming. Then the little prickly pear faces
smiled up from the sand at their clever cousin who had
already regained his innocent pose. I swung wide to
dodge one cholla but was almost unhorsed as the fiery
mustang lurched sidewise. A covey of Mexican blue
quail had exploded from the base of a treelike cactus in
a roaring blur of wings. They had taken refuge there
from the ever-present circling hawks.

"*Cuidado, hombre!* You weel make the forced land-
ing on a rock," snickered Pablo.

I swung my mount back into the trail—the trail to
yesterday. Yesterday, where today was forgotten and
atomic bombs gave way to flint-tipped arrows, where

no radios could blare raucous interference while the red men danced to appease the gods and the rainmakers chanted their age-old supplications to the carefree, sterile clouds. Yesterday, where the tribesmen dwelt in mud-daubed hogans and let the blue-trimmed government houses stand vacant and despised on the hillsides. Yesterday, where hearts and lives were blended in a simplicity that took no note of time and where a psychiatrist could not have found a neurotic complex though he searched a thousand phlegmatic minds and souls.

That was the trail which led to Bi-mah Begay and her magic carpet which linked the past to the present and the soul of a forgotten people to the libidinal stream of life. That was the trail which led me, somehow, close to the heart of God.

The drafty hogan where Bi-mah Begay dwelt was not one whit different from the hundreds of others which dotted the reservation except that it was situated on a high plateau, accessible only after strenuous effort of either man or beast. It looked out across the miles of blue sage toward the purple mountains. Near the doorway an ancient juniper stood triumphantly victorious over a thousand storms. It must have stood there when Don Juan de Oñate carved his name on Inscription Rock four hundred years ago. Desert junipers live on and on while nations rise and fall and empires crumble into the everlasting dust. Their roots somewhere touch the "fountain of youth" lost beneath the shifting sands of a long-dead past.

Before the old juniper sat a wrinkled Navajo woman as ageless as itself. Her arms might have been gnarled branches of the tree except that they moved more certainly.

As my horse topped out on the plateau, with Pablo's close behind, the old woman reached up and fastened a woolen thread to the loom which swung from the juniper limb. She sat on a woolly sheepskin and was reaching up over the two feet of a gaily colored rug exposed to view, slipping the thread in and out through the warp. Her eyes may have been too faded to see, or her ears too weather-beaten to hear, but at any rate she seemed unaware of my presence.

"*Halah' hodzah,*" I said. It was about all the Navajo I knew.

The old weaver never looked up. Her stolid hands moved deliberately to their intricate task.

I looked around. On the west side of the hogan an Indian youth was sprawled in the shade. I thudded to the ground beside my horse and, leading him by the reins, crossed the few yards which separated me from the reclining brave. I thought he was asleep until I noticed a black eye peeping my way from beneath the brim of a battered felt hat.

I tried my Navajo language accomplishment on him. "*Halah' hodzah,*" I said.

"Well, hello yourself," he grunted.

"Is that Bi-mah Begay?" I asked.

"I guess," he answered.

"Don't you know?" I persisted.

"She says she is."

"What is your name?" I patiently inquired.

"Diego," he said, and pulled his disreputable hat over his eyes to go back to sleep.

"Is Mother Begay related to you?"

"I guess," came the muffled response from the hat. "I'm her son."

I wondered dully if it was against the law to kill an Indian. Kit Carson did it. I ground-hitched my horse and walked over to where the old woman sat before her loom. Pablo was still sitting his horse watching her. I followed his eyes and caught my breath in astonishment.

I suppose that I have seen ten thousand Navajo blankets and rugs. I have seen the largest example of their weaving art, a huge blanket thirty-six feet long, twenty-four feet wide, that required two years in the making. I have seen the gaudy trifles which are used as tourist bait—for those peripatetic curiosity seekers who look for just three things in an Indian rug: it's got to be big, red, and cheap. I have held in my hands the exquisite "whirling logs" rug, the design of which is based upon the ceremonial sand-painting, and for which the weaver will ask—and get—$1,000. I have seen the *bayeta* rugs, brilliant with the red of an imported English baize which the Navajo women unraveled and wove into matchless design. I have run my fingers along the rough texture of the chief's blanket, distinguished by the bold, vertical stripes. I have seen the simple, unbordered blanket of one hundred years ago, woven in horizontal stripes and subtly colored with vegetable dyes, and which collectors are glad to get for $2,000 or more. But never have I seen anything so entrancing that came from the mind and heart and fingers of a weaver as the partial rug upon which Bi-mah Begay worked. She unrolled it from the loom, and I saw that it was almost finished. I could not take my eyes away The magnetism was unexplainable. Her beautiful art wrapped up my heart in an inexplicable way: I seemed to live over, as I gazed upon her handiwork, all the misty years of the forgotten and unknown past.

Could it be that a thread from her loom did actually link this old woman with the legendary Gallinas people? They were evidently pueblo dwellers, with their tower fortresses, while the Navajos were nomadic, trusting in mobility rather than in buttressed strength for their defense. But when did the Navajos become nomadic? Were they always wanderers of the desert? The questions tumbled over one another. I had no answer and wondered where, among the intricate designs of the rug, the erudite men of science could find one.

"Will you sell me that rug?" I addressed the words to the old weaver's back. She seemed not to hear. I searched my mind for a few Navajo words. I had spent some years in Santa Fe, New Mexico, and had met many Navajos. Two words came to mind. They were on the bottom of a post card which I had received once. They were *A-yo a-nos-nih.* I rejected them almost immediately. They mean "I love you." I was pretty sure as I looked at Bi-mah Begay's stiff back that they would not fit my purpose.

I nodded to Pablo to come with me and went back to where the Indian youth lay feigning sleep. *"Quiere usted este dollar?"* I shot a glance at Pablo and noted his approving grin. I held up the silver dollar and waited for the Indian's reply. I knew that most desert Indians understood Spanish. I was hardly prepared for what followed.

Languidly the youth pushed the old hat back from his eyes, revealing a finely sculptured and intelligent face. "What do I have to do for it, my typical white-friend-who-thinks-he-could-buy-a-piece-of-the-moon-for-a-dollar?"

I swallowed my consternation and grinned at him. "I just wanted you to tell me about that rug which your mother is weaving, and if it is the one I want, I would like to know how much it would cost me."

"There you go. All white men want to know how much anything costs. It never occurs to one of them that we Indians might not care to sell some things. I went to see the governor at the mansion in Santa Fe. He showed me all through his fine home. Everytime I saw a nice chair, I said, 'How much do you want for it?' He showed me some pictures on the wall, and I said, 'How much would you take for them?' We ate lunch together, and I asked him if he would sell me his silverware. He did not like that. Finally he said, 'You are the rudest Indian I have ever met. You insult me in my own home by wanting to know how much I will take for everything you see, as if I were a second-hand dealer on First Street.' I laughed at him. 'Now you know what we poor Indians have to put up with. You come into our houses, and you say of the rug on the floor, "How much?" of the eating pots, "How much are they?" And the governor—he's a good guy—laughed and said, 'You have taught me a lesson, and I shall try to pass it along to other white men and women.' Now, as I was saying when I so rudely interrupted myself, give me that dollar!"

I flipped it his way, and he caught it without ever looking toward it. He thrust the piece of silver down into his shallow jeans pocket.

"Let's go!" he said.

We approached the old weaver. Diego squatted beside her, took out his pocketknife and began to whittle. Finally he addressed his mother in Navajo. He seemed to be explaining my presence and object. She never turned her head.

I interrupted. "Ask her what those symbols mean which she is weaving into the rug."

The youth looked speculatively at me and gazed away across the rolling hills. Finally he grunted something at the weaver, and with the suspicion of a smile lurking at the corners of his mouth, he turned back to me. "Oh, they mean this and that; maybe this, and," he spat into the dust, "maybe that." It was high enlightenment.

Impassively the old woman continued her weaving.

Now, I know Indians well enough to realize that here was a situation which called for some Napoleonic tactics. I was tempted to yank the young man to his feet and demand my dollar back. I might have fared badly in the attempt. Besides, I would have failed. Indians may be shot with a degree of success, but they cannot be intimidated. As I watched the old woman's dashing hands, I reorganized my offensive. I determined to try to talk with her myself, reinforced by Diego's presence. I pointed to a curious design near the upper part of the rug and put the question.

"Qué es?"

The old woman did not so much as look up at me, but turned her head. I imagined I could hear her ancient neck squeak with the effort. She fired guttural sounds at her indolent son with the velocity of cannon balls.

"She says," the whittler interpreted with a curious smile on his face, "that it's a rug."

I had reached an impassé.

Moving over to the imperturbable jackknife artist, I resisted the desire to try to strangle him, and sat down on my haunches squarely in front of him. He moved his feet ever so little and whittled faster, the shavings flying over me like ashes. From the moment the young fellow had stood up back by the hogan, I had known that I had seen him somewhere. Then his use of good English and his familiarity with the city of Santa Fe, indicated that he had been in a government school. I had it! How could I have forgotten? Right half for the Indian eleven. I remembered him now. My own high school brother had called him "Swivel Hips."

"Diego," I said, apropos of nothing evident, "that was a great football game you played for the Indian School against the Miners, Thanksgiving Day a year ago."

The knife poised in the act of throwing another splinter in my face, and ebony eyes showed a spark of interest.

"Oh, yeah," he said, and I was sure he had been to college. "Did you see it?"

"Did I see it? Of course I saw it. And I know now why you were a guest in the governor's mansion. He was the best rooter in the stands. Say, that seventy-five yard run you made when you whizzed around left end and dodged through a broken field was one of the classiest things I ever saw. They should have made you All-Southwest Half for that."

"Say," cried the ex-football star, now thoroughly aroused, "that last Miner tackle almost nailed me. In fact, he did nail me, but I fell over the goal line instead of on the field."

I could hardly mask an exultant smile as we discussed that football classic, and I was grateful for the good fortune which had allowed me to see it. Gradually I led the Indian youth back to my interest in the blanket. I told him that his heritage of tribal warfare must have prepared him for the more effete game of football.

"Maybe," he grinned good-naturedly, and I knew that I had made a friend. I wondered a little about the poor, misguided white men who thought that an Indian would never talk. "We Navajos have always been considered a warlike people," said my new friend, "but we like to think of ourselves as peace-loving. We have fought, but it has always been to keep what was already ours, or to secure the things which would keep our people from starving. That rug which my mother is weaving is the history of our people when we lived beyond the mountains."

My heart skipped a beat as he got to his feet and

walked closer to the old weaver, motioning for me to
follow. He paid no attention to Pablo.

"My mother is telling our story, not as the white
man would tell his, with big, bragging words on paper,
but in the old, old language of our people—signs."

Then for nearly an hour the Indian lad talked, his
voice vibrant with indignation at times, and again
quivering with some deep, untranslatable sorrow. He
related the moving epic of his people with tenderness
and pride. He told how they had been peacefully dwelling in a cuplike valley between two mountain ranges
when the fierce Apaches rushed down upon them, kill-
ing and laying waste their villages. He pointed a stern
finger to the arrows woven with white wool into the
design, and said that they meant "fight." He showed
me other symbols representing faith in the Great Spirit,
fear of the demon gods, and finally a breathless
prophecy of the future when his people would be able
to live at peace with all men and to till their fields,
hunt, and fish in security.

My heart was lifted up as he talked. I forgot about
the degradation and starvation to which the Navajos
as a tribe had been brought, and my mind seized upon
a destiny for them that was dreamed of by no one save
perhaps an old woman who wove rugs and her lithe
young Bachelor of Science son who interpreted them.

"I want to buy that blanket for a university in the
East. How much will it cost?"

Diego looked for a moment as though I had slapped him. He became his old frozen self. "I am not so sure you could buy it at any price," he said, stiffly. "My mother is famous. She can sell any blanket she weaves for a lot of money. Sometimes she weaves one into which she also weaves her heart. Such a rug as the one before you contains Bi-mah Begay's soul. Such a rug could not be for sale." He was looking into the distance where the purple mountains were piled against the sky.

"Forgive me, Diego. I did not mean to be crude. The men whom I represent do not wish to treat your mother's work with irreverence. They are interested in the progress of human knowledge. Your mother seems to hold the key which will unlock a page of history for the enrichment of mankind. Perhaps you will let me come again to see the blanket. When will it be finished?"

Diego looked long and searchingly at me. "Perhaps," he grunted, and turned to leave, without answering the last part of my question.

"Please allow me one more question, Diego. Your mother interests me greatly. I can well understand that the craftsmanship of her heart cannot be bought with money. You are right about the white man. He seems to think that he can buy anything on earth with his dollars. Let us forget money for a moment and see if your mother will answer a question for us. Tell her first that I think her work is wonderful. Then ask her, for me, how she learned to weave so beautifully."

Diego put the questions in the hacking language of his people. For the first time the old weaver looked directly at me. She seemed to be studying my very soul. Her eyes were hypnotic in their stare. I felt a prickly sensation at the base of my skull.

Suddenly the harsh lines seemed to melt from her face. Her voice was low, and this time her son had to bend his head closely to hear her words. He turned to me.

"She says it is easy," he related. " 'The Great Spirit makes the sheep that roam the hills. Then I come along and catch that sheep. I cut off its wool. Then I twist the wool into threads. Then I color some of them. Then I weave the rug, and the Great Spirit and I have made the picture.' "

I bowed slightly to the wrinkled old desert artist. "Thank you very much," I said. For a moment she looked deep into me again, and satisfied with what she thought she saw, smiled at me and showed one stained tooth.

III

Tracing the Design

THE sun hung low over old Battleship Rock as we rode back along the trail. Beyond a ridge of sandhills a coyote yelped in the staccato rhythm of the chase, and I knew that a fleet-footed jack rabbit had laid his long ears back to streamline himself against the wind and was giving a good account of himself in the never-ceasing desert battle for existence.

"If I may be so bold as to ask the back of your neck, *señor, a donde vamos*—where do we go—from here? You have not the rug, and yet you ride."

I had totally forgotten Pablo. My first feeling of frustration had simply crystallized into a determination to possess the beautiful Navajo rug in the name of science if it could be had honorably and without offense to its weaver. I had simply ridden away in order to think. Pablo's question was entirely practical. We had supplies for a week and camping equipment in the jeep, parked by a tiny stream a dozen miles away. I reasoned that in a couple of days the rug would be finished. It would not be difficult to spend those days.

"Pablo, are you smarter than a fish?"

"That depends, *mi amigo,* on what kind of a feesh. I am smarter than the sucker, which weel try to take the worm off the hook weethout biting and swallow heem instead, and I am smarter than the carp, wheech tries to eat standing on hees head."

"How would you like to go trout fishing for a couple of days?"

"Until the old weaving woman she cool off a leetle bit and finish the rug?" grinned my irrepressible young friend. *"Bueno!* I weel show you how to lasso the trout weeth a horsehair loop tied to a stick."

"Pablo," I reproved, "that is against the game law."

"Maybe she ees," admitted the Mexican youth, "but eef the game warden, she theenk eet ees easy, I would like to see heem try eet."

"All right; you try a horsehair loop, and I'll stick to a Gray Hackle fly."

We rode on through the gathering darkness. The first stars had slipped out from the shrouds of the black desert sky. They seemed warm and friendly. No one has ever really seen the stars who has not ridden horseback through the desert night. I was thinking of David's paean of praise in the nineteenth Psalm:

> The heavens declare the glory of God;
> And the firmament showeth His handiwork.

God!

The Great Spirit!

The Great Spirit and I!

God—and—I! Not the "Meinself—und Gott" of an arrogant Kaiser launching a world war, but a holy, humble partnership of a lonely soul with the Master of the universe in the building of a better world! And I knew that the yearning of a wrinkled old desert artist, a ward of an alien government which had taken her fore-fathers' land, and the yearning of a small member of that same commonwealth, locked even then in a strug-gle against the forces of evil in world powers, were akin: we each walked after his own light, with God.

The thought came to me, too, as I gave my horse his head and let him trot along the trail that we are, all of us, weavers. Each has the same loom: the loom of life. Each has the same shuttle: the shuttle of time. Each has some threads at his disposal: qualities of mind and heart and spirit. Each in his own way, each in his own day, weaves his own pattern, for better or for worse. We do not all weave with the same degree of skill or conscientiousness. Some get the thread all tangled, knotted, or broken, and the ultimate design seems as lacking in sense as surrealistic art, while others, inspired by the guiding fingers of the heavenly Artist, weave the pattern beautifully and well. Rich or poor, foolish or wise, ignorant or learned, bond or free, strong or weak, male or female, white or black or yellow, red or brown—we belong to the ancient guild of weavers, and we trace out our designs against the backdrop of eternity.

What was it old Hezekiah said in the book of Isaiah, the major prophet? "I have rolled up, like a weaver, my life; he will cut me off from the loom." My mind, active with the strange events of the day, reconstructed that scene of the long ago. It was in the king's bedroom. The monarch was supposedly on his death bed. Looking down upon him was a stern-faced old fellow with eyebrows like black toothbrushes and eyes like tracer bullets. With the gentleness and tact of dropping a brick on a gouty foot, the old prophet shouted to the king:

"Set thine house in order: for thou shalt die, and not live."

I smiled as I thought of it. Though I had never seen a king die, I was pretty sure of one thing: a king becomes a democrat when he faces death, for death levels all mankind. The king and his subject inherit the same small square of dirt for a final resting place. A crown of gold would look ridiculous on the head of a corpse. Hezekiah acted like a child afraid of the dark. He turned his face to the wall and began to pray, "Jehovah, hear thy child. Do not let me die!" His quavering, childlike plea ascended with fear-winged feet the stairway toward the throne of God, who heard and graciously extended the king's life for another fifteen years.

In convalescence, the king was reflective. He had come very near to death, and in those hours his entire life had passed his mind's eye in quick review. He saw life as a mystic tapestry into which he had woven his dreams, his hopes, his ambitions, his joys, his despairs, his triumphs, and his failures. The design was about complete, and his part would be finished. Then God would cut the binding threads from the loom of earthly existence, and the tapestry would be hung in the halls of the Eternal, never to be changed, irrevocable, immutable. The king shivered.

My mind came back home. Each of us, like Hezekiah of old, is weaving. The great, immeasurable difference is this: we still have life. The inexorable scissors of God have not cut us off from hope. We still have time to fashion a better picture. Even a greater thought is this: we have a divine plan all blue-printed by the matchless Architect above, a plan with our initials on it if we will just take it for ourselves. We are not cosmic thistledown to be blown here and there by the vagaries of blind chance over the trackless paths of a haphazard universe; neither are we soulless automatons, wound up by an arbitrary superkey in the grip of a cruel fate and placed upon an iron-girt track which finds its consummation in limbo. We are free moral agents, following our own volition in a world which was given to us by a divine Creator to subdue and make conformable to his will and ours. We are partners with God—no less!

In this mechanistic, regimented age of goose-stepping robots, it is easy for any one of us to forget that we can stand up against the stream of social pressure and dare to be ourselves. It is even easier to forget that our lives have divine significance and are pertinent, even integral, parts of the economy of the universe; that we are not lost sight of, but that there is One who will guide and strengthen us for every time of need and will help to fit us into the Great Plan. The cosmos is not, as some hardened critics have affirmed, the delirium tremens vision of some celestial tippler, but is the intelligent conception of a wise, just, and all-powerful Creator. God is working out a masterpiece for the ceaseless aeons beyond the shores of time. He works slowly, building here, tearing down there. We cannot always trace his blueprint because we are a part of its lines. Our vision is necessarily blurred by our own shadow.

My soliloquy carried me back in memory to some of earth's most beautiful places. I rode down into the depths of the Grand Canyon on Bright Angel Trail. As the stolid mule, on which I sat more or less uncertainly, swung past an abrupt bluff, I reached over and extracted a piece of rock from a crevice. It was rough, and sandstone-like in appearance—just like any other common stone. There was nothing so wonderful about the Grand Canyon, I decided as I looked at the sand-stone and turned it over and over in my critical hands. The next morning I stood on Yavapai Point and watched the exquisite play of colors on the ageless temples and shrines below, carved and painted by the hand of God. I felt like removing my shoes from my feet as did Moses of old, confronted by the burning bush, for the ground whereon I stood was holy ground.

I walked down where the wavelets hissed along the wet sand and rolled back into the sea to be lost in the surge of the restless billows that washed the continents of the earth. I waded out into the cold water and dipped up a glassful of the ocean. It tasted brackish and salty, and looked very much like any other water. What was there about the ocean to make a man drive a thousand miles to see it? I asked myself. Just then I lifted my eyes beyond the rolling waves and saw the sun dropping like a gigantic orange into its hazy hori-zon line and I thought: "God has formed the ocean out of the driving clouds and it is good."

I stood watching the drip, drip, drip of tiny drops of water beneath the earth's surface. They carried with them muddy sediment. I wondered why tourists from a foreign land would cross the ocean just to see what I saw then. I was in an immense room nearly one mile in length, 750 feet below a New Mexico desert, but my eyes were fixed, for the moment, on the little drops of water dripping, dripping down. There was not much to the Carlsbad Caverns, after all. They were just a hole in the ground, worn there by the little drops of water, falling one at a time almost since the world began—a hole with slimy stalagmites standing on the rocky floor and equally slimy stalactites hanging from the dusky, bat-covered ceiling. These were all common things. But as I lifted my gaze toward the hazy heights in the distance and saw the rich magnesium flares lighting glory upon glory, palace upon crystal palace, I knew that this was the most uncommon thing of the physical earth, that only God would dare to dream into existence a wonderland like this.

This is the way life is. Taken moment by moment, it may not be inspiring. Considered alone, the individual human existence may appear totally irrelevant to the cosmic economy. Many a man has so rationalized his way to suicide. There is nothing quite so unbearable as uselessness. We must remember—we dare not forget—that God's great universe moves according to his plan, and in that plan we have a wondrous part. The individual life can be counted successful by the calendar of time only as it is true to its segment of that design.

The wrinkled old Mother Begay followed a well-executed plan as she fashioned her beautiful blankets and rugs, else they could have resulted in gunny sacks. Each of us, as he weaves the pattern of his separate life, must follow a plan of dreams, of prayers, of spiritual revelations, and careful thinking.

Though some acidulous realists object, dreams have their vital place in the forming of a well-rounded life. Every worth-while achievement in the interplay of human endeavor was born first in the soul of a daring dreamer. This dreamer was not some misty-eyed introvert who filled his mind with star dust and his heart with sawdust. He was one who was willing to match the outreach of his mind and spirit with the sweat of his forehead and the muscle of his arm. Before the first steamboat snorted its way into the pages of history, it danced from the spout of a hissing teakettle into the mind of James Watt and skipped into the vision of Robert Fulton; before the words "What hath God wrought" crawled from a copper wire into the unbelieving ears of a skeptic, the telegraph instrument was born in the mind of Samuel F. B. Morse; ere the voice of Alexander Graham Bell was heard in a telephone receiver, another voice spoke in the great man's heart and told him to keep on and on; before the first tungsten filament set a glass bulb on fire, its phosphorescence lighted the brain of Thomas Edison; long before Wilbur and Orville Wright saw their mechanical bird rise up over Kitty Hawk, it took wing in their own hearts—the story will not end until the earth itself does.

Anna Tozier sings so beautifully of dreams:

Last night they fluttered by me, as I sat in the gathering
  gloom:
With a golden thread I was weaving a song in a silver loom.

A-weaving the ghost of an echo of a rare and lovely strain,
As glad as a child's soft laughter; as sad as a cry of pain.

They followed my gorgeous fancy—my bark that idly goes
From a land that no man seeth to a land that no man
  knows.

My busy fingers faltered, as they hovered about my head,
And the wheel of my loom did slacken . . . I had broken
  my golden thread.

Then my soul leaped up to hold them—my dreams so wild
  and sweet,
And the golden thread unraveled, and the thread lay at my
  feet.

Each day I strive to weave it—this song that my soul would
  sing,
But I break my loom, and tangle my thread, and the tor-
  sions cling.

If they would but stay and teach me—if my dreams I could
  only hold,
I would weave in a loom of silver a beautiful song of gold.

But I strive in vain. They follow where the bark of my
  Fancy goes,
From a land that no man seeth, to a land that no man
  knows.[1]

---

[1] *Heart Throbs* (New York: Grosset & Dunlap, 1905), p. 420.

We shall not, as Anna Tozier reminds us, realize all of our dreams, but we are the better for our trying; a dream turning to ashes is better than no fire at all. "If you can dream—and not make dreams your master," says Kipling, you will be a man. It is interesting to note that Kipling considered dreams as stepping stones to manhood. But, as with every good thing misused, dreams are dangerous. There is the temptation to make dreams the end rather than the means of life, and to take refuge in a twilight world of unreality—the resort of neurotics. The escapist uses his dreams as a dope addict does cocaine, and with pretty much the same mental results. Dreams must not be opiates to drug the mind, but steam to drive the spiritual pistons of the human will. The world has always been changed by the mystic who embraced a vision and who packed within his own soul the fires to shape it into life.

It does not seem irreverent to suppose that God himself has dreams. Furthermore, it is not presumptuous to assume that men, though free moral agents in this universe which God has built, have a place in those dreams. That is to say that we shall realize God's plan for our lives only when our dreams coincide with his. This is what prayer seems to be, a merging of our dreams together. If God is the Father of his earthly children, he will not leave them orphans, he will tell them what to do. A prayerless Christian is a confused Christian, if not a downright absurdity. Prayer is the channel through which we receive God's blessings. How did Paul obtain the strength for life which he mentions in Philippians 4:13? Did God pour it into him in the way that a workman pours concrete into a wooden form? No. The apostle opened the floodgates of his heart to receive the streams of God's grace. Prayer is not a monologue directed toward God by a beggar who will not wait to hear a response. It is rather a spiritual walkie-talkie, two-way communication system with man listening as much as he speaks. Prayer is the absolute answer to every human problem. When the men of earth learn the secret of true prayer, they will not have to worry about the less potent effect of atomic energy let loose upon the world. "Prayer Changes Things" says the old wall motto, but it changes things by changing men.

The world of business knows many men, successful, resourceful, intelligent men, who would no more think of beginning a day's work at the office without a prayer to God than they would appear there without shaving, or dressed in their pajamas. Prayer to them is a vital, basic part of their commercial and personal relationships. No matter how rough the going may get, these men are never the victims of hypertension or nervous collapse. They are steadied men, guided men, men with a Partner.

God will show us the answer in every decision of life if we will only let him. I remember how a successful marriage began in the shadow of an old pine stump. Two young people sought me out at Inlow Youth Camp in the beautiful Manzano mountains of New Mexico, where I was appearing on the program. "We want to get married," said the young man, "and we are afraid. Can you help us?" I looked at him for a moment. "No," I said bluntly. His face froze, and he turned away. "Hold on a minute," I said. "I cannot personally help you, but I know someone who can. Let us kneel down here and take the matter to Him."

Together we knelt in the shadow of that old stump. I asked God to reassure their hearts and to show them the way toward a happy married life. I asked for his blessings to abide upon them. When I had said, "Amen," that lad whispered one sacred sentence, "O, God, *do* show us." His sweetheart whispered, "Amen."

Such a home could not fail. "Homes built upon prayer," said one divorce court judge, "never crack up in my court."

Jesus prayed constantly, not just in emergency, but with a devotion which marked it as an attitude and not an act. He never made a decision without asking his Father about it. If that was necessary for him, how much more needful is it for us, children of the dust!

Through prayer God will help us to weave the pattern of a life that will endure forever, a masterpiece for the galleries of the City Foursquare, of which we shall not be ashamed.

"Why do you not talk, *amigo*?" came Pablo's petu-
lant voice. My meditation had lasted for half a dozen
miles while my horse mechanically followed behind
Pablo's mount, in and out among the clumps of sage
and greasewood. Darkness had long since closed us in,
and to my left I could see the dim outline of a mountain looming against the stars.

"I have been thinking, Pablo," I replied, "about
such things as prayer. Do you ever pray, Pablo?"

"Me, I am a very religious man," came the solemn
rejoinder. "To *Dios* I pray every day. I pray like Jesus
did, for *tortilla* and *frijoles*. But I pray for somet'ings
more than food. I am pray for the world and the shape
she's een. I am pray that men might quit the fightings
and leeve together. I am pray that men might be
good."

"Does God hear your prayer and answer it?" I persisted.

"*Si, si señor. Dios* hear and answer. Maybe sometimes hees answer ees no, and maybe he say, 'Wait a
leetle while, Pablo,' but maybe those are answer what
I need. I theenk God know what he ees doing."

"Thank you, Pablo. You help me greatly." I meant
it. Pablo had the faith to believe that God called him
by name. He had the faith to look to God for everyday
needs. He knew the meaning of intercessory prayer for
his fellow men. He had the patience to wait upon the
Lord. Jesus phrased it differently in his answer to the

disciples when they asked, "Lord, teach us to pray," but his words meant the same thing. I had learned all over again that God is very real to many of the simple people who live close to the soil and the sun and the rain. He can be just as real to city folk who live a push-button existence, if they will just shut the world out a while each day and let him speak.

"Yo veo la jeep!" yelled Pablo suddenly, and I knew that the jeep was just ahead. I was ready for a night's sleep.

IV

The Red Thread
of Courage

"The Spanish Cavalier went out to rope a steer
   Along with his five cent *cigarro*.
'*Carramba!*' cried he, '*mañana* you'll be
   Muy buen carne for mio.'

"He bulldogged the steer, *con* nothing to *decir*
   And mounted, *otra vez*, his *caballo*.
Con gritos de glee, his sombrero donned he
   And *vamos* to the town to get *borracho.*"

"H EY!" I yelled as I thrust my head from the sanctuary of the sleeping bag, "why can't you let a fellow sleep? And what do you call that bilingual monstrosity you were murdering? I mean that alleged song which is neither Spanish nor English?"

"Ha!" snorted Pablo. "That song, she ees my own composition to show that I am the educated man what understands two languages. Are you going to eat the breakfast weeth me, or are you going to sleep all day like the burro?"

Shiveringly I crawled out of the sleeping bag and stretched my aching body. I stood transfixed in astonishment. I had stepped into the middle of a desert sunrise. To the east, long fingers of mauve were clutching at the lightening sky as though trying to pull back the gray curtains of the dusky half-light. Shimmering ribbons of gold were tied to the top of the needling peak behind which the sun still hid its ruddy face. The air was brittle with the lingering predawn cold, and my breath made tiny puffs of vapor. Before my enraptured gaze stretched the vast reaches of the Arizona desert, cold now, and vaguely mysterious. Chattering Mexican blue quail were coming alive in the greasewood thickets. The little stream which ran alongside the jeep added its many-toned song as it rushed down its rock-strewn bed on its way to the thirsty desert flats. Its source lay somewhere beyond the mountain range to the north.

"Thees bacon and thees *huevos* I am going to throw in the fire een just one meenute," warned Pablo, oblivious to my preoccupation with the beauties of God's wonderful world.

Never have I eaten a more delicious meal, prepared without benefit of stove or table. Never have I eaten in a more beautiful dining room—surrounded with real picture windows which changed their colors with every passing moment of the sun's upward journey into the turquoise skies. Pablo knew how to cook bacon, not so crisp that it was practically burned, but nice and juicy, and served with eggs that were flopped over and cooked lightly just so the yolk would barely run. The coffee would have elicited the praise of an old-time Texas Ranger.

After breakfast I jointed my eight-foot fly rod and attached a 2X tapered leader to the line. I knew something about wary rainbow trout in small, clear streams. Because it was early in the morning and the right time of the year, I attached a Royal Coachman to the tip of the leader and buckled my split-willow creel over my shoulder.

Pablo watched these preparations with ill-concealed disgust. "What weel you do eef the trout she ees too smart and weel not bite?" he demanded.

"I'll just eat some more bacon," I replied.

"*Tonto!*" snorted my friend. "But for me you would eat bacon. I weel catch some feesh. I do not have to wait for the trout to bite at a hook weeth some feathers on eet. I weel lasso heem weeth my leetle horsehair loop."

"And the game warden may lasso you," I warned.

Pablo just grinned.

Fishing was easy. I went upstream a couple of miles, fishing the riffles. In just two hours I had my limit of eight-inch rainbows and was trudging back toward camp.

Pablo lay sprawled under the shade of a large juniper. He had snared six beautiful trout in one hole not fifty feet from the jeep. That was enough for one meal; so he had knocked off piscatorial operations and had gone placidly to sleep. I did not awaken him, but cleaned my own fish in the stream and laid them in a pan which I wedged securely in some rocks at the water's edge where they would be kept fresh.

All morning my mind had reverted to the theme which had occupied it the night before. I kept seeing the old weaving woman and her magic rug, and I realized that she had begun to weave some kind of delightful spell over my own soul, using my heartstrings. I was wanting desperately to gather up the threads of my own life to weave them into a pattern after God's liking. I sat down in the jeep and surrendered my mind and spirit to meditation. There was something about Mother Begay herself, divorced from the work of her hands, which had gripped me. What was it? I remembered her as she looked, sitting there under the gnarled juniper, as though she were an instrument of the Great Spirit, her granite-like jaw outthrust, and her parchment skin stretched like old leather over her high cheek bones. I had it! The quality of character which had reached out to snap my mind into sharp focus was *courage,* glorious, triumphant, matchless courage—a courage to meet defeat without a whimper, pain without a cry, failure without despair, poverty without worry. Mother Begay had woven herself into the pattern on her loom with the bold red thread of courage.

"When the zero hour came for us to storm the German trenches," said a veteran of the First World War, "I was scared stiff. My legs refused for a long moment to move. My tongue was absolutely paralyzed, and I could feel my jaws working, but as though they were part of a machine far removed from me. My heart pounded like a hammer. I wanted to run, anywhere, just so I could get away—"

"Did you?" I interrupted.

My friend turned astonished eyes upon me. "Certainly not!" he said. "When the command came, I ran all right, but not away from Jerry. I would see some buddy fall with his body torn to pieces, but I went on. I was a coward, but I went on just the same."

I went on!

Not without fear, but with knees that trembled, my friend Tom went "over the top." He came out of the war with a chest full of medals. After one desperate action by American forces a war correspondent referred to Tom as a "man without nerves."

Tom called his fear cowardice. He was dead wrong. The difference lies in that calm, dispassionate statement: "I went on." Courage is not the absence of fear but mastery over it. The man who boasts that he is not afraid of anything might as well boast that he is a half-wit: something was left out when God put him together. A sense of caution is standard equipment for every man, and if he fails to have it, he is incomplete.

It is doubtful if there ever lived an individual totally devoid of some kind of fear; if of nothing else, he was afraid of being afraid. My fear may not be the same as another's, and, conversely, where he would walk without a quickened pulse, my own heart would turn to water.

The biographies of the great are the stories of their fears. Napoleon Bonaparte, Shakespeare, and Kaiser Wilhelm II were so afraid of cats that they lived in constant terror lest some innocent little furry kitten might be found in their bedrooms. Mohammed and Horace Greeley were terrified by loud sounds. Roger Bacon was a brilliant scientist and astronomer, but he was afraid of an eclipse of the sun. We read with amusement that the great biologist Charles Darwin shook with dread before the glassed-in cage of a harmless puff adder. Bayle, the celebrated French philosopher, from whom it is said that Voltaire got most of his ideas, was afraid of running water. The haughty Maria Theresa of Austria quailed before any human eyes and carried a sunshade to protect her from the stares of some humble subject along the road where her majestic carriage might be drawn.

Aside from the special phobias which lie within the

province of the psychiatrist, there are, broadly speaking, three kinds of fear which confront us all: physical, mental, and moral.

We all fear sickness and death, but we have somehow been able to build up the stamina to meet them. Bleeding, ragged, filthy British soldiers who escaped the death trap in Flanders marched into England with eyes that stared straight ahead, unseeing. One soldier whose hair had turned white because of the horror which he had witnessed said, "There came a time when we were no longer afraid. We were inured to pain and death and welcomed either." It is perhaps easier to conquer the physical fears which beset us than it is the mental.

The whole world today is mentally afraid. Military men insist that we are already in a third world war in which the objectives will be the extermination of entire continental populations. We still have the specter of Hitler, just a decade ago, in campaigns which lasted less than twenty days, swallowing up either in combat or in bloodless revolution in quick succession, Austria, Czechoslovakia, Poland, Belgium, France, and a half dozen lesser countries. Yugoslavia and Greece took a little longer. Looking back we realize with a shudder that he came so near to conquering Great Britain in 1940 that only his incredible blunder of failing to concentrate his attacks on vulnerable British war industries prevented his seizure of the world. Then Russia rose up in self-defense and stalled the mighty *Wehrmacht,* only to replace it with the mightiest army ever known to earth, and today we are at war again. United Nations men are dying—at the decree of Russia. Fear goes to bed with us each night.

Newspapers tell the daily story of fear, as suicides, afraid to live and less afraid to die, take the easy way out. Jazz and jitterbugs, liquor and alcoholics, gambling and dope fiends, promiscuity and broken homes, shallow parents and juvenile delinquency, forsaken churches and crowded prisons: evil companionships walk two by two in columns of death across the face of the land meant to be the "land of the free" but a land of slaves—slaves to gnawing, agonizing fear. The radio, motion pictures, television, hurtling automobiles, and the dance hall furnish escape to those who are afraid to sit down in quiet where they might have time to *think.* And yet, a greater weapon than her atomic bomb is Russia's big *idea.* If we become too afraid to think, we shall be smashed by a thought—for that is what communism is, just a lethal idea. The only defense against it is a bigger idea—soul competency! The right of any man to be a man, and not a state-controlled puppet.

Moral fears attack us all. There come times when we are afraid to stand up against the crowd. We are afraid of jeers, of threats, of criticisms, even of ostracisms inflicted upon us by the masses. We are afraid of such harsh words as "peculiar," "narrow," "fanatical," "bigoted," "prudish," and we sell our souls for praise.

If we are not afraid of the crowd and can successfully withstand the mob, we still quail before some individual. Peter could face the blood-thirsty ruffians of the Garden of Gethsemane with a human ear impaled on the tip of his sword, but he could not face a little serving girl who looked him in the eye and said, "Thou art one of them." Some of us who can go up against an enemy without a tremor, fall before the first wheedling note of a loved one.

There comes a time for most of us when we must stand alone, and see those who were our friends suddenly become our enemies. The Florentines who would have worshiped Savonarola as king burned him at the stake a short time later. The moral coward knows that and launches his little ship on the stream of "opportunism" or into the slough of expediency. He lives and dies and never leaves a footprint on the earth. He never has a quarrel because he assents to everything; he never has a conflict because he is never held by a conviction; he is a two-legged chameleon, fit more to inhabit a cage than a planet.

Who can save us from fear? Only the Man called Christ. He saves us by example, but by more than that. They called our Lord many things, but no one ever called him a coward. Tested by the three fundamental fears, Jesus was no physical coward. For forty days and nights in a barren wilderness with only the crows and the jackals to keep him company, he withstood the test of hunger that gnawed at his vitals. "Man shall not live by bread alone," he cried in the face of the devil. Once, with a knotted lash, he drove from the Temple of the Lord those who were profaning it by their merchandising. But it was on the cross that he showed men how to conquer pain. When his life was being torn from him in unbearable anguish, he scorned the anesthetic sop which would have deadened his pain a little, and died with a courage so great that it shook men from their graves, transformed the heavens into a tempest, and made the devils in hell drop to their knees and cry, "Surely this is the Son of God." A Roman centurion said, "Amen."

Jesus was not a mental coward. He dared to hurl his mind across the years, and his thinking fits this day in which we live as well as it did Pilate's. His Golden Rule is a surer guarantor of peace than all the mutterings of Lake Success, than twin stockpiles of atomic bombs in Russia and America that would reach to the moon! He was not a mental coward, and because of that somehow he walks today upon the earth where the international clouds of hatred and of strife lower upon the haunts of men, and whispers to those kneeling in the dark, "It is I, be not afraid."

Jesus was no moral coward. Looking the Pharisees levelly in the eyes, he challenged them, "Which one of you convicteth me of sin?" When the devil offered him the kingdoms of the world if he would bow down in worship of evil, Jesus lashed him with the cry, "Get thee hence, Satan: for it is written, Thou shalt worship the Lord thy God, and him only shalt thou serve." Jesus was no moral coward. He defied the world for a principle of life, and the world retaliated in the only way it knows to treat its greatest characters. Jesus steadfastly set his face toward Jerusalem, and just as steadfastly his enemies, the haters of truth, hewed at a wooden cross.

V

The Blue Thread of Strength

O NE thing I remembered as I thought of the wrinkled old Navajo weaver at work before her loom, was the feeling of vast strength which she seemed to impart to her work. As she drew the threads ever tightening in the loom, the muscles of her dark arms corded and flexed with a strength seldom found in a man's wrists and forearms. She appeared to have the endurance of the eternal hills around her.

And into the loom she wove that quality of herself, a toughness that made her hold on and on to a dream which she made to live. She was bound to her loom by a strong cord.

The thread of strength has four interwoven strands: physical, mental, moral, and spiritual.

Paul exhorted the men of Corinth, "Quit you like men, be strong." He must have meant that the badge of true manhood is strength. Conversely, then, to be weak is to be childish. It is certain that Paul's admonition embraced more than the mere physical. He did not mean that every man, regardless of his own physique, should be able to emulate the Roman gladiators in dexterity of combat. It just is not given to all of us to have the same physical stamina and power. We cannot be held responsible for a heritage which we never received. On the other hand, many an individual has wasted glorious physical energy in dissipation. Others have squandered magnificent physical powers in the mad scramble for wealth and position.

The Bible tells us that our bodies are the temple of the Holy Spirit. Then it must follow that anything which defiles the body makes it uninhabitable as God's dwelling place. The body is designed for exercise. If this be true, then physical laziness is a sin. Many an earnest preacher of the gospel, too busy about the Lord's work to get out into the country with a gun, a camera, a fishing rod, or a golf club, is not a martyr for Christ: he is just a sinner.

Jesus was a man physically strong. He was not the effeminate character visualized by Sallman. Isaiah knew more what he looked like. A sissy never would have thought of kicking over the tables of the money-changers and laying a lash to the thieves' backs; and if he had thought of it, he would have come to grief in the endeavor. A sissy would never have walked seventy miles over rugged trails in order to be baptized. A sissy would have died in one week of the temptation in the wilderness; and the strongest man reading these lines would be buried in three weeks, essaying to match the example of Christ. A sissy would not have had the question asked of him, as Mark puts it: "Is not this the carpenter?" It took a man to build an ox yoke.

A long look at John the Baptist with his leather girdle around his loins, his head back and his eyes flashing fire as he addressed himself to the "vipers" who knew no repentance, brings the conviction that here was a man with physical strength to match his words. And who could conceive of Peter as a physical weakling? Lloyd C. Douglas probably painted an accurate picture of the "big fisherman." The disciples who rallied around Christ were robust, virile, manly men. It took a man to lead them.

The old notion that to be physically weak was to be saintly was a heresy fostered by contempt and hatred for the people of God. If it is a mistake to enshrine weakness, however, it is no less an error to worship physical prowess. A football player is often an old man at twenty-eight.

There is another strength greater than the mere physical. It is power of mind. Here, again, no one of us is accountable to God for that which he never had. We are not expected to use the brain of an Einstein, but we are supposed to use the brain which God gave us. Einstein cannot think as clearly about spiritual things as a farmer's wife can who chugs a churn dasher with one hand while she reads a Bible held in the other. Einstein could give to the world the theory of relativity, but he could not speak ten sensible words about the relationship of a mortal man to the God who made him. We need not despair at our lack of mental equipment, but we ought to put to effective use that which we do have.

The kingdom of God needs citizens of mental strength to combat the erroneous thinking of a groping world. They need great wisdom, and wisdom is a gift of God; knowledge is merely acquired. God allows Christians, under the leadership of the Holy Spirit, to think his thoughts after him. What greater wisdom can there be than that?

The world in which we live needs citizens who will dare to think. Dictatorships are possible only when the masses of men become too lazy to think for themselves, when they would rather surrender their minds to another. Creative, meditative thinking is almost a lost art to those of our generation. It is easier to listen to a narration over the radio and have our thoughts predigested, or to visit the movies and have them siphoned into our craniums. And with the coming of television sets to upwards of ten million homes, we have even less use for our minds. If the mind of the average man is not to become stultified and his brain to become a vestigial remnant like his appendix, that average man had better begin to exercise his gray cells.

The brain needs exercise, but it needs healthy exercise. Paul put such mental exercise into the closing chapter of Philippians:

Finally, brethren, whatsoever things are true, whatsoever things are honest [honorable], whatsoever things are just, whatsoever things are pure, whatsoever things are lovely, whatsoever things are of good report; if there be any virtue, and if there be any praise, think on these things.

Man is the only member of the animal kingdom endowed with reason. For him to be mentally lazy, then, is to repudiate his own origin. The hardest work in all the world is mental labor. That is why so many shun it. We can do physical labor to the point of exhaustion and recuperate our strength rapidly, but when we exhaust ourselves mentally, it is exceedingly difficult to make the comeback. Most people escape this problem simply by yielding to mental inertia. They use their minds as little as possible, and in saving them, lose them in bare utilitarian service—just enough to get by. Such people really do not live; they simply exist. Life is too precious for that.

Mental strength comes not only by exercise, but by concentration. I caught myself not long ago listening to the radio while I shaved with an electric razor and read a book at the same time. That is ridiculous. And yet we are so conditioned to noise that we can't read or sleep without it. It is no wonder that we have grasshopper minds that flit here and there without restraint or profit. If we could learn to concentrate on one thing until we thought it through, we would become wise enough to inherit the earth. At least it is worth trying.

More to be desired than all else is spiritual strength. A physical giant can wreck society; a mental giant can wreck the world; a moral giant can change men's lives. But a spiritual giant can lift the world toward God. Sometimes a man can have due portions of all four. They complement one another.

It is related that "Gentleman Jim" Corbett, the most romantic figure in pugilistic history, was walking through a crowd on a busy street when a roughneck jostled him, then whirled around and shouted, "I have a notion to slap your face."

The impeccable Corbett bowed and smiled slightly into the other's eyes. He said, "I beg your pardon. The error was mine."

The ruffian shouted, blissfully unaware that he was addressing the heavyweight champion of the world, "Watch where you are goin'. Next time I'll smash you one."

A friend followed the fighter away. "Jim," he said, "why didn't you knock that smart aleck down? If you had hit him once, his head would have rolled a block. Instead of that you were as polite to him as if he were a woman."

Gentleman Jim is said to have replied, "I can afford to be polite because I have the punch to back it up."

The Christian, with the moral reserves of the universe back of him, can afford to be polite. He does not need to resort to sarcasm, cynicism, anger, or revenge in his dealings with his fellow man. He certainly does not need to walk with "a chip on his shoulder."

Sarcasm is the attribute of moral weakness. Someone has said that "sarcasm is the refuge of little minds." And it might be added, of little men. It is easy to be sarcastic about motives which we do not understand, ideals which are above us, convictions which we have never owned, and truths which we cannot answer.

Cynicism is another quality of moral weakness. It proclaims us as supreme egoists, all wrapped up in our own small minds. The cynic is a coward because he has already surrendered to his own disbelief in God and in his fellow men. He would destroy by his supercilious contempt the faith of another simply because he has no faith of his own.

Anger, too, is moral weakness. Whatever else may leave us untouched, here is the battleground of every soul. If a man's greatness is measured by the importance of the thing which makes him angry, some of us belong in the "rogues' gallery." In the state where I live, state traffic laws give the pedestrian the right of way over a vehicle on any intersection. Recently the newspaper carried the story of a motorist driving down a busy highway when a pedestrian stepped out from the curb to make his way across to the other side. The pedestrian was wholly within the rights granted to him by state law. The motorist stopped all right, but he jumped out of his car, ran up to the pedestrian, and started hitting him in the back with his fists. He came to with a black eye, his car snarled in a traffic jam, and a police citation in his hand. Anger usually gets us just that far.

Revenge is another ingredient in the makeup of moral weakness. It is a loaded gun, but pointed in the wrong direction. Revenge always hurts the one who exercises it more than it does the recipient. Revenge is honey for the moment, but it is wormwood through the years. It gives us great satisfaction for the time being to know that we have brought to his knees one who has done us wrong, to see him crawling in the dust at our feet, but that satisfaction gives way to our own contempt for ourselves that we could have stooped so low. If we could just remember that if a thing has been done to wrong us, it has wronged God more, and he is able to take care of himself! "Vengeance is mine: I will repay, saith the Lord." That ought to be enough.

One other thing needs to be said about the things which destroy moral strength: the greatest of these is hatred. Hatred and strength can never be bedfellows. Hatred is the most enervating of human passions—and the most inexcusable in the child of God. Hatred belongs in the jungle, not in the paths of civilization.

And that is exactly where it will take mankind if it is not stopped: back to the flint-tipped spears and the caves of the Stone Age. Man will either learn to live upon the earth without hatred, or he will not live on it at all.

It is not necessary to point out that the crying need of our day the world over is for such men of moral strength as Josiah Gilbert Holland described in the familiar lines:

God give us men! A time like this demands
Strong minds, great hearts, true faith and ready hands.
Men whom the lust of office does not kill;
  Men whom the spoils of office cannot buy;
Men who possess opinions and a will;
  Men who have honor—men who will not lie;
Men who can stand before a demagogue
  And damn his treacherous flatteries without winking;
Tall men, sun-crowned, who live above the fog
  In public duty and in private thinking;
For while the rabble, with their thumb-worn creeds,
Their large professions and their little deeds,
Mingle in selfish strife, lo! Freedom weeps,
Wrong rules the land, and waiting Justice sleeps.

The fourth strand in the cord of strength is spiritual. The author of all human strength is God. "I will lift up mine eyes unto the hills, from whence cometh my help," cried David. The shepherd king looked beyond the hills to God.

The beginning of spiritual strength is a surrender of heart and will to Christ. Spiritual power cannot begin where sin is growing. Jesus alone can rid a man's heart of sin. Is this old? Is it passé? Is it archaic? Then where else, how else, has it ever been demonstrated on the earth that a man can live above sin?

Physical strength is greatly to be desired, mental strength is to be coveted and to be won, and moral strength is to be counted precious, but these are not enough. Jesus pointed out that the rich young ruler, who was a moral giant, a keeper of the law, a better man, negatively, than anyone who will ever read these words, yet lacked something: self-surrender to God.

The beginning of spiritual strength, then, is surrender. To be born again is just to yield to the will of God. What is repentance but that? It is a forsaking of the things of the world for Christ. It is being crucified to the world, as Paul said. It is a change of attitude toward sin. It is putting oneself at the disposal of God. And this is surrender. Repentance is not something which we achieve for ourselves: it is the gift of God, the Bible says. What is faith but surrender? The same Bible says that faith is the gift of God. When we yield to the will of God, that is all!

If salvation is the beginning of spiritual strength, it is certainly not the end, any more than natural birth is the end of physical life. Spiritual life begins with the new birth, but it does not end there. Spiritual life is growth in the things of God. Paul made this clear when he talked of spiritual babes, who must suckle, and spiritual adults, who can eat with a knife and fork.

Spiritual growth is attained by faith and works, and the two are inseparable. We prove our faith, as James says, by our works. Prayer is an act of faith, but it is also a work of righteousness; Bible study is a work of righteousness, but it is also an act of faith. Soul-winning is the greatest work of righteousness of them all, but it is also the greatest evidence of faith.

The life in tune with God, and only that life, is spiritually strong.

VI

The Golden Thread
of Faith

"THE Great Spirit and I have made the picture."

Again I saw the old weaver in my mind and felt her probing look into my own heart, as though she sought for some kinship of soul. Hers was a primal, complete, simple faith in the Power back of the universe. Hers, too, was a confident faith in herself as one counted worthy to be a partner with that Spirit.

The apostle Paul and Bi-mah Begay were continents and years apart, but they were met together here. Listen to the apostle: "We are labourers together with God." Now hear Bi-mah Begay again: "The Great Spirit and I have made the picture." Such faith transcends the composition of a Navajo rug; it is enough for the spiritual tapestry of life.

Three strands are entertwined in the thread of faith: faith in ourselves, faith in our fellow men, and faith in the eternal God.

On a hunting trip in New Mexico I found myself on a large cattle ranch which covered more than a hundred sections. I was walking along a canyon trail when I suddenly came upon an adobe shack occupied by a filthy-looking individual who was engaged in dumping dirty dishwater out of his front door, where it ran in a stinking little rivulet down the arroyo bank. He stood swishing a vile rag around a greasy dishpan as I approached. The man's hair was matted with dirt and looked as though it had not been combed in years. He swept me up and down with his bleary eyes as I spoke to him.

"Seen any deer?" he asked.

"Just a few does," I replied. "Say, how about a cup of coffee? Have you got a pot on the stove?"

"Yep; always have a pot of java. Come on in."

As I blew on the coffee to make it a little less blistering, I engaged my nondescript host in conversation. I had not talked with him five minutes before I realized that he was no ordinary ranch hand. He spoke excellent English when he tried.

It is an ancient rule of the West that a stranger not get too inquisitive about a man's past. That rule is still invoked in the wide-open ranch country. However, my curiosity was great, and I felt reasonably safe from bodily harm as I broke the rule because a high-power rifle rested across my knees. I complimented my host on being a man of some learning. He laughed bitterly.

"Graduate of Cornell," he said.

In my astonishment I involuntarily exclaimed, "Why under high heaven have you buried yourself out in these mountains to stagnate and decay?"

Then came his story. He told it as though in the telling he got vast relief. The day that man was to be graduated from the university, his best friend eloped with his betrothed sweetheart. In bitterness the university graduate began to distrust and actually to hate every other man he met. In time he hated himself. He also began to hate God. Unfit for life, he became a sullen recluse of the hills, and for twenty years had degenerated into the character who sat before me with his matted hair and dirty face.

No man ever succeeds until he has faith in himself. If he does not believe in himself, no one else ever can believe in him. He is a useless bit of driftwood on the eddying current of existence. This is not to say that he must be conceited or overinflated with a feeling of self-importance. But he must believe that he is in the world for some purpose which he alone can fulfil, and he must address himself to that God-given task with self-reliance. A man dare not fail God nor be faithless to his destiny. There are two magic words which are the "Open sesame!" to life: "I can."

"I can," said Thomas Edison. And while the office force stood around him in laughing scorn, the youthful

inventor turned the crank on an impossible contrap-
tion and spoke into a horn while a cylinder covered
with tinfoil revolved backward:

"Mary had a little lamb,
Its fleece was white as snow—"

And in a squeaky falsetto the horn replied as the
cylinder was turned toward the right,

"Mary had a little lamb—"

It was all because a young man said, "I can," and
did!

"I can," said David Livingstone, and mapped a
route from the interior of the darkened continent of
Africa to the sea. "I can," he said, and smashed the foul
slave traffic which had brought England to disgrace.

"I can," said Paul, "do all things through Christ
which strengtheneth me," and lifted Europe to the
throne of God.

A second strand in the thread of faith is belief in
our fellow men.

When I was a fifteen-year-old lad, I went to deliver
an order of groceries from the store where I worked
during the summer. I entered through the service
porch of a certain house and was just setting the box
down on the kitchen table when the woman of the
house appeared in the inside doorway. I stepped back,
startled. She was unkempt, her stringy blond hair fall-

ing in her eyes and over her shoulders. She was wrapped
in a sloppy housecoat. Her eyes were staring.

"Boy," she snarled, "does your father own a gun?"

I swallowed, tried to step backward from the appari-
tion. "Yes, madam," I gulped; "he has a forty-five."

"Then, take my advice, go right home and blow
your brains out!"

"Why?" I squeaked.

"Because life is not worth living. It is just sorrow
and disappointment. Your best friend will stab you in
the back. The one you love will come to hate you.
Everything you try will come to nothing. Don't ever
trust anybody." Her voice trailed off as I finally managed to back through the doorway.

Sad is the spectacle of one who has lost faith in his
fellow man. His defeat is certain. It is our common
experience to have those whom we have trusted prove
false. It is our common experience to be slandered,
maligned, and abused by those whom we have loved
and whom we have sought to help through the years.
It is common experience for us to be lied about, mis-
represented, and misunderstood. So, too, did they treat
Jesus—only worse! Which one of us has ever been
nailed to a cross?

Elijah had put to the sword the prophets of Baal,
but the wicked queen Jezebel chased him so far into
the wilderness that he crawled into a hole. Thereupon
he decided that everybody in the world was a crook,

save him. God had to tell the prophet that he had seven thousand men who had not bowed the knee to Baal. God still had use for Elijah, and he could not use a man who had lost faith in all others.

I changed trains in a little western town. It was early morning, and I walked along the deserted street, breathing in the crisp, fresh air.

Before a closed drugstore an old man was setting up on the sidewalk a queer contrivance of boards and wire. He was placing on display behind the wires the various newspapers which he sold. At one side was a little box with a slot in its top and a tiny sign saying, "Drop in your coin and take your paper."

The gray-haired old fellow got the rack adjusted to his satisfaction and without so much as giving me a glance, started to walk away.

"Wait a minute," I called. The man came back and looked at me quizzically from behind ancient steel-rimmed glasses.

"I've been looking at this rack of yours. What is to prevent me from taking a paper and not leaving any money? I don't see any kind of trigger-works or gadget to keep me from stealing one of your papers."

"There is one gadget, young man," he replied in his quiet drawl.

"Where is it?" I demanded. "I certainly do not see it."

He moved over and tapped me on the chest. "It's in

there," he said quietly. "It is called a conscience." He turned to leave, but I called him back a second time. "Now what?" he asked, with the suspicion of a twinkle in his kind old eyes.

"Surely you are not trying to tell me that in this hard-boiled world you would trust your entire stock in trade to the consciences of people whom you do not know!"

He said: "Young man, in 1907, about the time you were born, I lost all that I had in the great cattle panic —a $300,000 ranch in this very country. I came to town flat broke, and the owner of that hotel over there gave me $1.65. I built a newspaper rack just like this one. Later I built more. Today I own that building right behind you. I have a nice home and a new car. My son is being graduated from college this spring. Just remember this, son: a man is never out until he loses faith in others, in himself, and in his God."

I was then the editor of a country newspaper in New Mexico, and I wrote the story of the news vendor by way of editorial. The Pecos, Texas, newspaper printed the story in full as the editor's tribute to a leading citizen. It pays, in every way, to keep faith with those who travel with you life's uncertain pathway.

The third strand in the thread of faith links the human soul to God. Pitifully poor is the man who knows not God; exceedingly rich is the man who has all his needs supplied according to the riches of Christ in glory. His heart is fixed, and he stands secure on the foundation which is laid, which is Christ Jesus.

The Greek word for man, *Anthropos*, means one "who looks upward." Actually it is precisely that quality which distinguishes man from all other creatures of the earth. He alone can project his mind beyond earth's limitations; he alone worships an unseen Presence.

It is only when man belies his heritage and refuses to look upward that he wrecks his own life and brings the lives of others to shambles at his feet. Wars are launched, always, by men, and modern wars are perpetrated only by men who have forgotten God.

During World War II, when the hearts of millions were broken and despairing, one unbeliever sneeringly asked Dr. George W. Truett, "If there is a God, why doesn't he stop this war?" The great preacher answered quietly, "You ask me why God, if there is a God, does not stop this cruel war, and my answer is, he does not stop it because he did not start it."

There is no better answer. The horror conflict in Europe then was the product of so-called "scientific" thinking, which did not take into account any Word from God. Friedrich Nietzsche's was the philosophy that distorted the diabolical mind of Joseph Paul Goebbels, that actuated the reign of terror by the Gestapo of Heinrich Himmler, that inspired the mass murder of women and children by the air fleets of

Hermann Goering, and that set on fire with the lust to destroy one Adolf Schiklgruber, alias Hitler. These infamous leaders were members of the human race, and they listened while Nietzsche whispered: "To do evil is the true virtue, to be good is the most hopeless vice. We should live dangerously; and as material life is the power to digest poisons, so true excellence is the power to commit all manner of crimes, and to survive." They listened while he insisted, "If there were gods, how could I endure it to be no god? Therefore there are no gods." They forgot to listen to his babbling in the madman's room at Weimar. They forgot and they are dead, every one of them. But with them are ten million other corpses of those sacrificed on the altar of man's worship of himself. To forget God, then, is to die.

Though we cannot read entirely the mind of God, one thing is certain: the gentle teachings of the Man of Galilee never inspired any war. Think of them:

Blessed are the meek. . . . Blessed are the peacemakers. . . . Blessed are the merciful. . . . Whosoever is angry with his brother without a cause shall be in danger of the judgment. . . . Whosoever shall smite thee on thy right cheek, turn to him the other also. . . .

These comprise an ideology, too, but they never sent men to war.

Today the shadow of another mighty conflagration

lights up the skies of man's tottering world. America has a stockpile of atomic bombs, the most terrible instruments of destruction ever devised by the mind of man. Russia has a stockpile of atomic bombs, and the world waits to see who will throw one first. American and United Nations soldiers died on the battle fronts of Korea without benefit of atomic weapons. They died in the hope that, somehow, an atomic war might be prevented. For there can be no real defense against atomic bombs. Scientific men know this, whether military men do or not. We feel a little safer since our pile of bombs is higher; but deep within our hearts we know that only God can save mankind from annihilation, and he cannot do that against its will. Only in the shadow of a cross can peace be found, not in the shadow of a mountain of atomic bombs. The greatest army for peace in all the world is the missionary army, seeking to win the men of the earth to Jesus.

Faith in God, though, is not the property of a government, of a nation, of a commonwealth. Faith is the possession of the individual soul which has renounced sin in repentance and surrendered itself to God through faith in Christ, his only begotten Son, who died on the cross to set men free from the law of sin and of death.

VII

The Violet Thread of Love

MOTHER BEGAY had woven her very soul into the beautiful rug on the loom before her, said her dark-skinned son solemnly, and added that one does not sell the product of one's heart. Therein lay the secret of the exquisite beauty of Bimah Begay's masterpiece: it was woven with the fibers of love.

My close friend of a score of years, Colonel Wilfred McCormick, the author of the famous "Bronc Burnett" series of boys' books, had created a character in young Bronc Burnett that was wholesome and entirely lovable. Bronc piloted a small-town baseball team to dizzy heights of fame. Not only was he a baseball star, but one of football and basketball as well. He was a youth of sterling moral qualities and clean sportsmanship. Church leaders all over America, realizing the need for such idealistic books for boys, saw to it that the Bronc Burnett series was included in their lending libraries.

As Bronc Burnett skyrocketed to fame, he attracted the attention of a certain movie producer who offered his creator a fantastic figure for the movie rights to the books. Colonel McCormick asked: "Will there by any drinking scenes in the picture? Will there by any profanity?"

The movie producer said, "Who ever heard of a ball team which did not have some of both?"

"Then," said my author friend, "I am not interested. You see, I consider Bronc Burnett exactly as though he were my flesh-and-blood son. I am not going to sell him to the movies and have his moral character weakened."

A wrinkled old Navajo weaver fashioning a beautiful rug, a cultured ex-army officer creating out of his own heart the image of an all-American boy—they were somehow akin. Both knew how to love the deeper things of the soul. Mother Begay could weave the wondrous epic of her people only because she loved them. Colonel McCormick could tell the story of Bronc Burnett and a boy's baseball team only because he understood and loved boys.

The old song has it that "the world is dying for a little bit of love." It is not true. The world has a "little bit" of love. It is dying for want of a lot of love. This is not to confuse love with sentimentality. The silly sentimentality of the modern song hit would gag even a

Pollyanna. By the same token, the silly sentimentality of some types of preaching would nauseate Christ.

The Master of men was arrested by the cry of a beggar somewhere in Galilee. A hideous-looking leprosy-eaten travesty of a man cried out to Jesus beseechingly as the Lord passed by, "If thou wilt, thou canst make me clean." And Jesus, moved with compassion, put forth his hand and touched him, and said to him, "I will; be thou clean."

"He touched me!" cried the leper. Wonder, awe, astonishment, a glad leaping of the heart, how these must have surged through every fiber of his being! Long, cruel, hopeless years had passed since he had felt the touch of another human being. All this time he had been forced to huddle to himself, crying, "Unclean! Unclean!" lest passers-by get too close. But now, for one blissful moment, he feels the touch of another being, and into his own poor body flows cleanliness, and into his broken heart flows love.

"She kissed me!" cried the painted, fallen woman of the streets who lingered for a moment after a Salvation Army service. Evangeline Booth had been speaking to her about her soul but could kindle no interest. Suddenly the glorious woman of God bent over and kissed the woman of sin on the cheek. Lifting a faltering hand to the flesh which had felt the imprint of holy lips for the first time, the poor woman began to cry with rack-ing, tearing sobs, "Talk to me now about a Christ who can make a woman like you. I am ready to listen!"

These two illustrations serve to point up the need of every human being upon the earth: for personal, sympathetic, physical human contact. It costs so little effort to shake a man's hand with a grip that communicates deep interest. And that handshake may save his life from wreck.

Between trains I once found myself walking down a part of State Street, which is the "skid row" of Chicago. A human derelict walked up to me with shuffling step, sized me up quickly, and said, "You are a Westerner." With something of astonishment I admitted it, wondering how he knew. I did not have on cowboy boots, my hat had been purchased in Nashville, and my suit looked just like any other man's.

A man better versed in the ways of the twilight world would have walked on. For that matter, any man possessed of good sense would have. Instead, I asked, "How in the world did you know?"

A gleam came into the other's faded old eyes. "I can spot 'em," he said. "Now, would you be hailing from New Mexico?" My astonishment rooted me to the sidewalk.

I admitted to residence in "the Land of Enchantment," whereupon my disreputable chance acquaintance informed me that he used to railroad out of a certain New Mexico town. Then came the denouement. "Say, pardner," suddenly whined the man, "will you stake me to a cup of coffee and a hamburger —just because we both come from the same state?"

I fished in my pocket for a quarter. I had had that much entertainment. But suddenly I saw beyond the man's animal-cunning. I saw a human soul crying out for help. I saw stark naked loneliness.

"Here is a quarter," I said, "but I am not giving it to you because we came from the same country. I am giving it to you in the name of Christ. I am a Christian."

The man stood looking at the shining quarter in his hand for a long time. When he looked up again at me, tears had streaked his grimy cheeks.

"Here, take your quarter back. I didn't want it for something to eat. I needed a shot of liquor. Take it back!" he fairly screeched, as he thrust the quarter back at me.

"Keep the quarter, fellow," I said, "but don't spend it for liquor. God will help you."

My skid row acquaintance turned swiftly with the quarter still held in his hand. "Mebbe there *is* a God," he muttered, "and mebbe he *will* help me."

I gave that nameless man much more than a quarter that day. I reached into his shriveled old heart and planted a seed of hope in God.

It is easy for Christians to profess a love for others in an abstract sort of way, but it is exceedingly difficult for Christians to show real love in actual physical contact with those who are surpassingly unlovely. It is easy to get sentimental over the black man in Africa, but hard to love the black man on our own doorstep; easy to worry about the plight of the starving Chinese and remain untouched by the pitiful cry of the city slum on the other side of the tracks. Such is our indefensible hyprocrisy.

Love is the most personal thing on earth.

Underlying all evangelism must be a divine compassion, kindled in the hearts of men by the vision of Christ, who loved enough that he *gave*. Without a longing so deep that it is painful, so agonizing that it is unspeakable, we might as well save our breath when we speak to a man about Christ or the welfare of his own soul in the light of eternity. The words which we speak are empty and impotent if they are not charged by the power of a breaking heart. No matter how eloquent and rhetorically correct the sermon, says Paul, it is like the rattling of tin pie plates together if it is not fashioned out of love. These are not the apostle's exact words, but they are his exact meaning. If we love enough, it might be added, we do not even need words.

My first experience in trying to win another to a decision for Christ stands out vividly in my memory after more than a score of years. During a revival meeting in our church the visiting preacher asked us all to promise that we would speak to some individual that very week about the Way of life. Even as I made the promise, fear clutched at my heart. That fear grew as the days of the meeting slowly passed. I could not summon the courage to make good on my promise. Came the last service of the revival and the last verse of the invitation hymn. I closed my eyes and prayed that the Lord would show me someone to whom I could talk. When I opened my eyes, they were drawn as though by a magnet toward a young fellow of about my own age standing next to the aisle across from me. What could I say to him? What arguments could I use? I fumbled for my New Testament and opened it to John 3:16. At least I could read the Scriptures.

With fast-beating heart, I slipped over to the young man as unobtrusively as I could. I had never seen him before, but suddenly I was overwhelmed by a great love for him. As I reached up to touch him on the shoulder, I felt hot tears scalding my eyes.

The young man turned. He saw the tears. I never said a word. Neither did he. Before I realized what had happened, he was on his way down to the front of the church to the preacher, and there before the altar of the Lord, surrendered his heart and life to God.

That is what the Bible means when it says:

He that goeth forth and weepeth, bearing seed for sowing,
Shall doubtless come again with joy, bringing his sheaves
   with him.

In such a time as this of international stress something needs to be said about the catalytic effect of love upon the world's disunity. It seems to be impractically and hopelessly idealistic to talk about brotherhood, common justice, and love in an hour when the armies of the earth are fighting the preliminary skirmishes of the third world war. Who, any cynic would ask, would want to send a valentine to Stalin, when a bullet would be more in order?

Let me state here that I am not a pacifist. I would shoulder a rifle in defense of freedom just as quickly as I would take it after a mad dog which threatened the safety of my children. On the other hand, I am not a militarist. I *do not* believe that the problems of the world can be solved by laying our atomic bombs on Peiping, Moscow, and the strategic centers of military installation of world Communists. We may have to do just that. Only one man in the world knows whether we shall or not; and that is Josef Stalin, and he is not talking! Whether that day comes or not, one thing is certain: the world cannot be welded together with atomic fire. There is a power greater than the sword, and that is the power of love. Jesus made that clear to Simon Peter in the garden of Gethsemane.

From the First World War there comes a story by Dr. E. Y. Mullins which challenges the thought of any thinking individual:

During the course of battle a young British aviator brought down a German flyer. As soon as he could, he went to the fallen plane; and from the broken wires he drew the body of a boy about his own age, with a frank face and brown eyes. The heart was still. In the fallen boy's pocket was the picture of a gray-haired woman. It bore a name and address; and the British boy knew that she was the mother of the boy he had killed. He dug a grave for the German, buried the body, and marked the grave. Then he wrote this letter to the mother:

I am writing you about your son. I want you to know that I killed him. I know you can't forgive me. I want you to know that he didn't suffer. The end came very quickly. He was very brave. He must also have been very good. He had your picture in his pocket. I am sending it back, though I should like to keep it. I suppose I am his enemy, yet I don't feel so at all. I'd give my life to have him back. I didn't think of him or you when I shot at his machine. He was an enemy, spying out our men. I couldn't let him get back to tell the news. It meant death to our men. I know you must have loved him. My mother died when I was quite a little boy; but I know what she would have felt if I had been killed. War isn't fair to women. God! how I wish it was over. It is a nightmare. I feel that if I could touch your boy he would awake and we'd be friends. I know his body must be dear to you. I will take care of it and mark his grave. After the war, you may want to take it home. My own heart is heavy. I felt that it was my duty.

From the face of the mother, the British boy thought that she might write to him. She did. Here is her letter:

DEAR LAD:

There is nothing to forgive. I see you as you are, your troubled goodness. I feel you coming to me like a little boy, astounded at having done it, when you meant well. I am glad your hands cared for my boy. I would rather have you than any other touch his earthly body. He was my youngest. I think you saw his fineness. I know the torture of your heart since you have slain him. To women, brotherhood is a reality. All men are our sons. This makes war a monster, that brother must slay brother. Yet women, perhaps more than men, have been to blame for this World War. We did not think of the world's children. Our children, the baby hands that clutched our breasts, were so sweet that we forgot the hundred other baby hands that stretched out to us. And now my heart aches with repentance. When the war is over, come to me. I am waiting for you.

Such is the alchemy of God's love: it transmutes hatred into compassion and binds human hearts together with chains which transcend earth.

VIII

The Green Thread
of Patience

My MIND drifted back to Bi-mah Begay at her loom. I remembered her face as she impassively guided the thread through the variegated woolen warp. It was as immobile and expressionless as one of the granite boulders at her feet. In fact, it seemed to have been a part of that particular landscape forever. For a baffling moment I had been seized with the obsession that all of the pulseless ages of the past were being reviewed behind those inscrutable, washed-out old eyes.

It was the face of one who had suffered much. Pain, through many years, had drawn sharp lines down from the corners of her mouth. A thousand bitter disappointments had left their inevitable marks upon her leatherlike countenance. I looked in vain for any sign of weakness, for any sign of yielding to despair. Instead I saw only a straightforward acceptance of fate and the will to carry on. So might Job have looked as he cried out for a chisel so he could write his faith in lead in the rocks of the earth.

Among the resources which God will provide for every faithful life is the green thread of patience. Why green? I have called it that because green is the most restful color on the earth. The world is filled with greenness—the grass of the pastures, the crops of the fields, the trees of the forest, and even the waves of the ocean as churned by wind and rain. God has surrounded us in the natural world by a color that could bring us rest.

And if any generation ever needed to learn how to rest, we are it! We rush madly as Jehu down the crowded thoroughfares of our existence. Like syncopated phantoms we are now here, now there, hardly pausing long enough to eat. We begrudge ourselves the time it takes to sleep. We seldom, if ever, take time out to meditate, to read the Word of God, to pray, or to familiarize ourselves with the words of the great. The mighty Shakespeare has been neutralized into a comic book for the freewheeling brains of subway riders. You can even buy the Bible at the corner newsstand all dressed up like Buck Rogers so the modern father can understand it well enough to read it to his kids. A recent magazine of national circulation shows the picture of one of the most popular preachers in America, who times his sermons (the article says) by popping a cough drop into his mouth when he begins and saying, "Amen," when it dissolves. The article also implies that he almost preached a sermon one time when he popped a button into his mouth and it did not dissolve! He knew the patience of his own congregation, or, for that matter, of almost any other.

The apostle Paul challenges us to "run with patience the race that is set before us." How can one run with *patience*? Surely not the one-hundred-yard-dash man. He must click off a hundred yards in less than ten seconds, or stay at home. It is comparatively easy to understand how the half-miler, or the miler must set his stride to his endurance and hold himself in for that last imperceptible burst of speed which will break the tape before his competitor's brawny chest beats him to it, but what of the high-speed man? His, too, must be the stride which never varies in its machinelike regularity. The apostle, however, was not thinking so much of the competition itself, but of the intense and grueling preparation for the race, which is as much a part of it as the cinder track or the starter's gun. Meals at the training table; hours and hours and hours of torturing practice; abstinence from indulgences which will dissipate or impair the energies; and, finally, running the race only after one has become fit to tackle it—it was of these things the apostle was thinking. Paul would have frowned upon the young man and woman so anxious to launch out upon the stream of active career life that they quit school half-prepared for any specific task. He was also describing the propensity of most of us for leaving a work half done.

On the campus of Northwestern University at Evanston, Illinois, stands a memorial tablet erected by the alumni, bearing the following inscription:

In Honor Of
DAVID THOMAS HANSON
Arts 1905–Med. 1909
Captain Medical Corps 142nd Infantry
United States Army
Cited by the French Government for Bravery

"AN OFFICER OF GREAT COURAGE, AT ST. ETIENNE, Oct. 8, 1916, HE RUSHED TO THE AID OF A WOUNDED MAN AND WAS KILLED. HE WAS A MODEL OF DEVOTION."

Awarded the Croix de Guerre after death
A student beloved of his associates, generous, persistent, self-sacrificing.
He gave himself without reserve to his alma mater and to his country.

"HE PLAYED FOUR YEARS ON THE SCRUBS— HE NEVER QUIT."

Somehow, among all the heroic accomplishments of this hero of the First World War, the thing remembered longest by his classmates was the fact that "he never quit," though he could not make the first string on the football squad. And, after all, it may be exceedingly more difficult to stay with the scrubs throughout a college career than to die in a single blaze of glory on the battlefield. Captain Hanson matched his physical courage with a dogged moral stamina. He was doubly a hero.

Hear the story of the cowboy and the mud dauber:

The cowboy was in a line shack far out on the range. Awakened one morning by the splashing of the dawn in his face, he saw a mud dauber busily engaged in building its nest against a pine *viga* supporting the flat dirt roof of the adobe hut.

"Get out of my house, you ornery little dive-bombing cockroach!" he yelled, and hurled his boot at the buzzing insect's nest, bringing it crumbling to the floor. The startled little wasp zoomed down in a power dive, and the cowboy ducked under his blanket.

The next morning the cowboy rubbed the sleep out of his eyes, yawned, and—his mouth flew wide open in amazement. There was the little wasp busily at work on another nest of mud. The range-rider reached up to where his forty-five hung in its worn holster at the head of the bed.

"All right, you pesky little 'dobe-mixer! I told you to keep out of my house. Now, you can just take the consequences."

The cowpuncher squeezed off the trigger of his trusty old "hog-leg," and the mud dauber's nest exploded in a shower of dust and pine splinters.

"I guess that'll larn ye," he gritted, and put his revolver back into the holster with sweet satisfaction.

The next morning the cowboy jerked upright in his bunk in glassy-eyed consternation. The little wasp was back at work on its nest of mud and had it almost finished.

"Well, by the beard of the unlamented Pancho Villa de Mejico!" cried the exasperated cowhand. "Which of us is the stubbornest, you or me? I've broke broncs on nearly every spread west of the Pecos, and I'll scratch you, too, you mudslinging little beast!"

He threw another boot and demolished the nest, muttering to himself like a man demented.

The next morning—but let the cowboy tell it:

"I knocked that dirt-daubing sheepherder's friend out of business every morning for nineteen straight days, and gave up in disgust on the twentieth. I actually got to feeling sorry for him. I finally named that sky-hopping tumblebug 'Lil Abner,' and we became fast friends. I allus did like a feller that didn't know when he was licked!"

It is more than passing strange that a lowly mud dauber could preach such a sermon!

From a lowly mud dauber to Thomas Edison seems an absurd mental leap. But they had much in common.

It is said that Thomas Edison left his laboratory one day during the course of his experiments which produced the incandescent bulb, and his face was creased in a smile. An associate, knowing how hard the famed scientist had been working, and how many times success had eluded his efforts, shouted gleefully, "Mr. Edison, you have succeeded! I can see it by your face."

The giant of the world of science looked at his colleague speculatively. "On the contrary," he said, "I have failed again. But at least I have found seventy ways it *can't* be done."

Patience is the thread which ties mighty dreams to realities.

Not only is life a race, according to Paul, which should be run with patience, but it is a battle which must be fought with endurance. "Thou therefore endure hardness, as a good soldier of Jesus Christ," he warned young Timothy. To the vacillating Galatians he proudly said, as though he had just been awarded the Purple Heart by his Supreme Commander, "I bear in my body the marks of the Lord Jesus." Then, with his gray head bent for the executioner's sword, he whispered triumphantly, "I have fought the good fight."

In the warfare with Satan in which Christ's soldiers are engaged, there must be no faltering, there must be no crying out, there must be no fainting in the heat of the engagement. Crippled, we must struggle on; wounded, we must crawl forward; dying, we must not quit.

Into every worth-while life must be woven the green thread of patience by the Spirit of the living God.

IX

The Black Thread of Sorrow

NEXT to the splashes of bright red the most predominant color on Mother Begay's loom was black. She was unsparing of the somber background. Whether the color had some deep significance, either religiously or historically, I never learned. Its artistic value I never questioned, for it was revealed to my more or less uneducated eyes. Of one thing I was certain: without the black, the design would have lacked boldness and harmony.

Dark colors give tonal qualities to a picture even as deep notes give symphonic power to a musical composition. The great composers undergirded their masterpieces with bass voice; therefore they live. For life itself is built upon the deeper things.

We purchased an old pipe organ for our church. It had been installed in another edifice the year of my birth. Its tones were mellowed by time. I became deeply interested in the procedure of installing it and assembled a large part of the organ myself, since I had helped to dismantle it in the first place. Everything went more or less smoothly until I came up against the foot pedal arrangement which allowed the playing of thirty giant bourdon pipes. A microscopic hole in an air tube caused the pipes to cipher. I did not worry much about the matter because I knew that pipes that large could only grumble with the sound of a rushing wind, and that, in my judgment, would add nothing to the beauty of the music. Hence, I blithely left the bourdons disconnected.

Finally came the day when the organ was completely assembled. I could hardly wait to call the church organist and get her down to the sanctuary to try the instrument. The decorative pipes looked so impressive, towering up to the ceiling and swinging down in a symmetrical arc!

The organist joined me in a rapturous contemplation of the huge old organ completely filling the space back of the choir loft. "It is beautiful," she exclaimed.

She sat down at the console and flipped the switch, listening to the rumble of the air building up pressure as a mighty motor whirred in the basement. Then came the first notes of the organ. They were somewhat sour, for the organ needed the tuning touch of an expert. To me, though, it was the prettiest music I had ever heard. Suddenly I saw a startled look cross the face of the organist. She glanced down at the foot pedals with a frown. The music abruptly ceased.

"What's the matter with the bourdon pipes?" she cried.

"If you mean those big pipes, I didn't even connect them. I tried blowing in one and could not get a sound. I finally decided that they could not possibly contribute anything to the music. They would just make a sound like the wind blowing down a fireplace chimney."

"Those pipes have to be connected," quietly answered the musician. "I will not play this organ without them. Lacking the bourdons, there could not be balance to my music. I must have the deep tones whether your ear can hear them or not. They are essential to good harmony. When they are connected, I shall try the organ again."

That pipe organ was symbolic of life. The deeper notes sounded in our sorrow and our pain are necessary to harmony. No soul has become beautiful until it has suffered. In the crucible of life the dross is burned away and the gold is revealed. Job, sitting on the ash heap, covered with boils, with wealth and loved ones gone, a mocking wife in the background, answered the three all-wise critics sitting cross-legged before him: "He knoweth the way that I take: when he hath tried me, I shall come forth as gold."

Paul knew that to suffer graciously was to be Christlike and prayed in one of the most audacious prayers on record that he "might know him, and the power of his resurrection, and the *fellowship of his suffering,* being made conformable unto his death."

One of the most effective young Christian women I have ever met is one whose heart was broken during her college days. Disappointed in a love affair through a parent's interference, she took exactly the opposite course to that taken by the university graduate who buried himself in the mountain fastnesses of a western state to stagnate and decay. This young woman came to our little town as a high school teacher. As so many unwisely do, she attempted to forget her frustration in a mad whirl of social pleasures. Her health and mind were threatened.

One afternoon I found opportunity to talk with her and gradually drew from her, reluctantly, the full story of her wrecked life. I asked for the privilege of praying with her; and though we were in a public place, we bowed our heads and I quietly took the matter to the Lord.

"That is the first time I have prayed since it happened," she said, with a catch in her voice.

Shortly afterward this young school teacher went home for summer vacation. Before she caught the train that night, she slipped a piece of paper through the mail slot of the weekly newspaper where I was editor. There were a few words of thanks and the delightful poem by Helen Welshimer, "Consolation." I pasted the copy of that poem in the front of my Bible a score of years ago, and it is still there. Long since I wrote it upon the tablet of my own heart. It tells of triumph over suffering.

> So proudly now I'll hold my head
> As each tomorrow comes,
> That those who look at me will think
> I walk to singing drums.
>
> And maybe some of them will say
> They wish that life would be
> Just half as gay and nice to them
> As it has been to me.
>
> If they should bring me little griefs
> And little dreams to heal,
> I think that I could help because
> I know the way they feel.

There was one time upon the earth a "man of sorrows, and acquainted with grief." His face was marred by much suffering. He came unto his own, and they that were his own received him not. In fact, he was despised and rejected of others as well. He took upon himself, this one who knew no sin of his own, the form of a sinful man and became as a servant, obedient to death, even the death of the cross. He was numbered among the transgressors and crucified between two thieves. The people sat and watched him die. They shot out their lips in scorn. They mocked him. They railed against him. He asked for a drink of water when his suffering had reached beyond what any man could bear, but none gave him water to drink, not even Barabbas, the robber-chieftain whose place he had taken. In the blackness of the noonday night, he cried out, "My God, my God, why hast thou forsaken me?" There was no answer. God had turned his back, and this One on the cross was in spiritual death for a while.

In all this, the man said not a word of condemnation. He even prayed for his enemies. He was an example before us too great for any of us to follow. But we can try. And in the trying, we shall win a crown, for "if we suffer, we shall also reign with him." When the tapestry of each individual life is unrolled in heaven's gallery, we shall understand the meaning of our tears, "for," says Paul again, "I reckon that the sufferings of this present time are not worthy to be compared with the glory which shall be revealed in us."

X

The White Thread of Righteousness

I HAD noticed that as the old Navajo weaving woman worked her thread through the loom, she was unsparing of the white. It was the sustaining outline of every figure, the field upon which the design took shape. There is something beautiful about fluffy white woolen thread. It speaks of purity.

Around, and about, and through every immortal life there must be woven the white thread of personal righteousness. It has become fashionable for the hedonistic sophisticates of this age to sneer at personal religion. The old theology has been cast on the ash heap of supposedly unnecessary concepts of life. The "gray life" composed of white *and* black has become more desirable to the denizens of the modern world than the pure, white character enjoined upon us by the Word of God. Chastity has become a subject for parlor jokes and cocktail ribaldry instead of a personal, priceless, irreplaceable possession. To call the man of today a saint would be to invite a punch in the nose.

All this notwithstanding, the good life is still devoutly to be desired and, in spite of a world which has lost its balance, is still obtainable. Once in a while in our sane moments, we pause to give thanks for men who cannot be bought.

A recent news release brings to light a heart-warming story. Andrew C. Ivy, Ph.D., M.D., D.Sc., vice-president of the University of Illinois, is the discoverer of at least two hormones and heads a staff of thirty-five full-time research scientists at the University of Illinois.

Dr. Ivy was offered $100,000 to write a series of articles on beer and vitamins. He turned it down. He did, however, have time to accept the position of chairman of the National Committee for the Prevention of Alcoholism.

In a recent address Dr. Ivy said: "I regard it as sheer intellectual dishonesty to discuss the food qualities of beer, including its vitamin content."

Here stands a man who is not for sale for $100,000, but who will tell the truth for nothing. May his tribe increase!

The attitude of such a man as Dr. Ivy is completely mystifying to the average citizen of this nation; he seems to be a martyr for something totally unimportant. That a man, any man, should place such a high value upon personal integrity is as strange to the insensitive mass mind as a ritualistic burnt sacrifice in a South Sea Island voodoo orgy would be.

It is time we stopped short and listened to God, who said: "Righteousness exalteth a nation; but sin is a reproach to any people." My own generation has seen America go to war three times, without solving a single human problem.

General Omar Bradley, a fighting man, took an intimate look at the world and made a few pithy remarks which stagger under the weight of their own meaning. Says the general:

"Our knowledge of science has clearly outstripped our capacity to control it.

"We have too many men of science; too few men of God.

"We have grasped the mystery of the atom and rejected the Sermon on the Mount.

"Man is stumbling blindly through a spiritual darkness while toying precariously with the secrets of life and death.

"The world has achieved brilliance without wisdom; power without conscience.

"Ours is a world of nuclear giants and ethical infants."

That is an accurate diagnosis. How about the remedy?

That remedy is simple: the hearts of men must be changed, for it is men who make up the world. Too long have we hacked away at the branches of the tree of evil while ignoring its taproot. We rail against war and say that it is wrong, that it is immoral, that it is evil. War can be none of these. It is not wrong and it is not right; it is not immoral, nor is it moral, but it is completely amoral; it is not good and it is not evil. Only men are right or men are wrong, and it is men who fight wars. The Pope wanted to have the secret of the atomic bomb destroyed on the grounds that it was evil, but though the head of the Roman Catholic Church claims infallibility in his pronouncements upon moral questions, he missed the whole problem here. An atomic bomb is simply a machine—a material thing—not even necessarily of destruction. It has no volition, no mind, no heart; but its maker has all three.

When the men who foment wars come under the influence of Almighty God, wars will cease forever— but only then. Sentimental talk about the universal Fatherhood of God and the universal brotherhood of men is sheer nonsense. We become the children of God, and, therefore, members of his family through faith. We can become brothers only at the cross of Christ, where we renounce our sin in repentance and surrender our will to Christ. If that way is too hard, there can be no hope. Either we shall be saved by the blood of Christ, or we shall drown ourselves in our own.

If this sounds suspiciously like the old theology, that is precisely because it is meant to be.

Man is a sinner by nature. He inherited a tendency to sin from Adam, transmitted down to him through the stream of life. That is the doctrine of original sin, held to be so repulsive to squeamish contemporary thinkers. But a hesitating look at Dachau and Buchenwald, of Second World War infamy, will reveal that no amount of education, no wealth of culture, no indoctrination of science, no heritage of philosophy, can erase the savage which dwells within us. Germany was perhaps the most highly educated, the most cultured, the most scientifically advanced nation upon the earth, but it still wrote the greatest horror chapter of all history. The sin of Adam is inherited, and only one man ever lived upon the earth without it, the God-Man, Christ Jesus, born the "seed of a woman" with none of Adam's blood in him. That is why Jesus, called in the Bible the "second Adam," had to be offered up in death. He was "the Lamb of God," said John, "which taketh away the sin of the world." Sin here means the very essence of sin and not the acts only.

It follows, then, that man is a sinner in practice. He is not a sinner because he sins, but he sins because he is a sinner. That is his nature, and his deeds are merely the manifestation of it. As the plum tree brings forth plums because that is its nature, so man brings forth natural fruit according to his sinful nature. What Christians call the "new birth" or "regeneration" is really the birth of Christ in the human heart which has become surrendered to him. Paul says that "if any man be in Christ, he is a new creature: old things are passed away; behold, all things are become new." Our righteousness, then, is not of ourselves, but it is of Christ.

Man is not only a sinner by nature and by practice, but he is a sinner through deliberate choice. There are two ways set before him. One way leads up and the other down. Two personalities beckon to him: one is Jesus, and the other is Satan. Two destinies are open to him: one is eternal life, and the other is eternal death. Either the man will elect to follow Christ as a member of the family of the second Adam, who knew no sin, or he will elect to follow the way of the flesh, of the family of the first Adam, who took what he wanted and gave nothing in return.

The white thread of righteousness, then, is woven by the shuttle of self-surrender, and the white robes of heaven are reserved for those who have been washed in the blood of the Lamb.

Here is the invitation of God: "Come now, and let us reason together, saith the Lord: though your sins be as scarlet, they shall be as white as snow; though they be red like crimson, they shall be as wool."

From a lonely island in the Aegean Sea a white-haired man in exile addressed letters to the seven churches of Asia. To Sardis, with its social sins, its love of luxury, and its pleasure-bent members, he wrote: "Thou hast a few names even in Sardis which have not defiled their garments; and they shall walk with me in white: for they are worthy." There are always a few in every crowd who will dare to live close to Him. They are in the world, but not of it. Like the curious little

spider of South America which has the power of forming a bubble about itself, in which, like a diving bell,
it sinks to the bottom and remains for hours, yet is
perfectly dry upon coming up, so it is with the children
of God: they breathe the air from above even while
living upon the earth.

One other word needs to be said. The white life is
not a colorless life, the saintly one not an uninteresting
experience.

A Hollywood producer gave an item to the newspapers in which he said, "There is no story in the life
of a good woman." How low can a man sink?

No story in the life of a good woman! French soldiers
on Flanders' bloody fields cried out to Joan of Arc, the
sweet maid of Orleans, to save them. But, says this
movie producer, there is no real story in the life of
Joan of Arc because she was a good woman! There was
no story in the life of the mother of Moses, hiding her
child in a pitiful basket among the rushes and waiting
anxiously until she was assured of the care of Pharaoh's
daughter for her son! There was no story in the life of
Deborah, who fought with more strength than any man
for the salvation of her country! There was no story in
the life of Mary, the mother of Jesus, who gave to the
world its Saviour though her own heart was broken!
There was no story in the lives of Jane Addams,
Frances Willard, Florence Nightingale, Evangeline

Booth, or your mother or mine. Those were good women.

This is the insidious psychology which Hollywood uses to undermine morals for the sake of dollars. Contrary to the flippant statement of the movie producer is the fact that the good life is the adventurous life. It takes more courage to walk the high and lonely trail than it ever does to drift along with the crowds on the lower levels of existence. The clean life is the heroic life, victorious over self. It takes more real manhood and womanhood to follow Christ than it does to engage in any other activity upon the earth.

Then let us move confidently toward this great adventure: walking in white with Jesus.

XI

The Woolen Thread of Simplicity

Out in the vast Arizona desert, where the wind and the rain had carved ship-like sails from the indurated structure of the granite mountains and set them to float upon the billowy waves of sand, out where the skies of turquoise blue folded their diaphanous canopy above the serrated ridges of purple ranges; out where streams sang their many-toned songs as they rushed toward oblivion below; out where a cluster of mud-daubed hogans faced east toward the rising sun, and an Indian mother sat weaving —there in the companionship of a half-wild Mexican youth I found a simplicity which spelled *happiness*.

Bi-mah Begay was happy for a fundamental reason: her wants were few and easily supplied. Apart from the hissing torrents of human life she sat where the current smoothed into lazy eddies, where a fellow human being a dozen miles away was yet a neighbor.

Frenzied individuals the world over are rushing here and there earnestly seeking for an elusive and transitory quality of mind and heart which they call "happiness." But even in the seeking they lose the object of their search. For happiness is not something which can be sought and won; it is not a fortress which can be assaulted and conquered; it is not fashioned of "things." Happiness is a by-product which comes in forgetting self. It is most easily found in the simple life.

F. W. Boreham, the Australian bush preacher and essayist, points out the fallacy in the little prayer taught to children:

> Gentle Jesus, meek and mild,
> Look upon a little child!
> Pity my simplicity!
> Suffer me to come to thee!

"Why 'pity my simplicity'?" asked Boreham.

It is the one thing about a little child that is really sublime, sublimity and simplicity being ... everlastingly inseparable. Pity my simplicity! Why, it is the sweet simplicity of the little child that we all admire and love and covet! Pity my simplicity! Why, it is the unspoiled and sublime simplicity of this little child of mine that takes my heart by storm and carries everything before it. . . . It outstrips me, transcends me, and leaves me far behind. It soars whilst I grovel; it flies whilst I creep.[1]

Just as a picture which is otherwise admirable is spoiled by too much detail, just as a tapestry that would otherwise be a masterpiece is marred by an intricacy

---

[1] F. W. Boreham, *Mushrooms on the Moor* (New York: The Abingdon Press, 1919), pp. 148-9.

that wearies the mind, the human life which is garnished by inordinate wants, desires, and satiations becomes confusing in its impact upon others and unwholesome to its possessor. The simple, consecrated, and concentrated life is the happy life. If you do not believe it, examine the biographies of important men and women.

Paul said, "This *one* thing I do"! We must not scatter our mental, physical, and spiritual resources among too many earthly projects. The life with a worth-while goal *and that goal in constant view* is the successful and the happy life.

The simplicities and the sublimities of a soul in tune with the Infinite are the ingredients of a happiness which endures. We should never become too busy to enjoy the raptures of the simple things, for, while we seek life, it will pass us by.

There is an old story told by Phillips Brooks, the master Boston preacher. He was visiting in a certain home just before he was scheduled to deliver an important lecture. After luncheon little time remained, just enough in fact to make a hurried dash for the place where the lecture was to be given. As he was making quick preparations, a little child came near and said, "Mr. Brooks, you must see my little kittens before you go." The lovable preacher did not hesitate, but said with endearing simplicity, "Well, my dear, if I must, I must!" And then, following her pattering little feet, he went down a dusty stairway into a dingy cellar and whispered to her about her kittens as he lifted them up one by one. Just one hour later, men and women were swayed by his oratory and sobbed under his power. He had time for the simplicities; he rose to the sublimities.

When I read that story, I thought of a certain real-estate man in our town who tried to sell me a house.

"This house," said the hard-boiled real estate broker, "is $10,000. Of that amount, you would have to pay $2,000 down—."

"Mister," squeaked a small voice, "do you know what to do with a horny toad?"

The man looked down. A freckled little hand clutched at his coat. The owner of the hand looked upward, expectantly. His other arm was around a gallon bucket, which he hugged to his breast.

A tiny girl, her eyes sparkling with excitement, chimed in, "Yes, Mister, do you know what to do with a horny toad, huh?"

Half a dozen children had been milling about in the yard when we drove up. Now they were quiet, listening intently.

Forgotten was the real-estate deal and the $500 profit to him if the sale went through. Forgotten was I, the potential customer. The big real-estate operator reached quickly into the bucket. "Sure, I know what to do with a horny toad." His hand came out, and the horned toad was on it. The little girl gasped. The boys squealed with delight.

"Watch me make him go to sleep," said the man. He spat out his huge cigar, and his face softened. "Now, watch."

He gently rubbed the vicious-looking little lizard on its bristly, barbed head, holding it all the while on his big left hand. The lizard's eyes closed. The children stopped breathing.

"My goodness!" whispered the little girl.

"Put him on my hand," the boy demanded, while the little girl looked on in glittering-eyed astonishment. Then, with an unmistakable swagger, the freckle-faced boy marched toward the back yard with Little Bright-Eyes at his side and the other children following in jabbering excitement.

"Now, where was I?" asked the real-estate agent as he turned back to me and the business in hand.

"I know where you are, now," I answered him quietly. "You are in the heart of a certain little freckle-faced boy."

The real-estate man looked at me quickly, then looked away in embarrassment. Finally he spoke. "That means more to me than 5 per cent," he said.

If we could cultivate the simple things of life, the fruit of our garden would be unending joy. We should bring happiness to others and, in doing that, find it ourselves.

We need to nourish our hearts on the simplicities. Nature can show us the way. A desert weed that has been spun round and round by the sultry winds until it has marked a perfect circle in the sand . . . white, fleecy clouds drifting across the face of a mountain . . . the smell of newly turned earth in the patter of summer rain . . . a clump of daisies beside a hillside rock . . . sweetheart and wife sitting by the fire reading with the cat curled along the arm of her chair . . . a cluster of violets amid lacy ferns . . . a mountain brook murmuring happily toward the sea . . . dark forms of trout leaping up the falls . . . the solemnity and extravagance of a western sunset splashed across a darkening sky . . . the eternal ebb and flow of tides sweeping across the beaches, leaving hissing little bubbles and crackling seaweed in their wake . . . a hummingbird streaking like a bullet against the dogwood blossoms . . . a squirrel sitting on the limb of a spruce holding a piñon burr in its paws and gnawing as fast as its tiny incisors can cut . . . mallards sweeping up against the dawn . . . a baby playing in a sand pile talking to playmates you cannot see . . . sunlight tiptoeing through the stained-glass windows of a sanctuary . . . sweet old organ music in the shadowy twilight . . . a wrinkled old Navajo weaver fashioning the pattern of a matchless rug on a homemade loom and weaving threads of gold about your heart. . . .

XII

A Matter of the Heart

"EEYOOH!"

The eerie sound penetrated the flap of my sleeping bag, and I came to with a start. My skin prickled. Very cautiously I leaned over and peeped under the tentlike head canopy. It was broad daylight. The air was nippy.

The irrepressible Pablo squatted on his heels before the cheerful campfire. He deftly flipped a pancake high into the air and caught it on the battered skillet, letting out another bloodcurdling whoop at the same time.

"Eet ees *mañana!*" he yelled. "The day ees made for work, not for sleep. Today we go get the rug, *que no?*"

I wriggled from the bag, rubbing the sleep from my eyes. "What a dainty and considerate way to wake a fellow up," I reproved, as I stretched my aching muscles. "Don't try that panther scream on me again, or you might get shot."

"*No puede tirar*—you can't shoot," grinned Pablo. "You do not have the gun."

"Oh, no? After breakfast I will show it to you. It's in the jeep."

"Why you deed not get the gun yesterday and keel us one *conejo* so we could eat somet'ing *bueno*?"

"You are burning that pancake," I reminded him. "If I shot a rabbit with *that* rifle, there would not be enough left to pick up. It is a 30-06."

"That ees nothing. Me, I have the 30-30 at home."

"My rifle makes a 30-30 look like a popgun." I could not resist the opportunity to impress my young Mexican friend; so while breakfast waited, I pulled on my shoes and went over to the jeep. In a moment I had a beautifully carved leather case in my hands. I carried it fondly over to where Pablo squatted by the fire. He was eyeing the case curiously.

With just the proper dramatic touch I drew from the case my most prized possession. As the sunlight glinted on the polished blue steel of the rifle barrel and shone on the velvety, oil-finished walnut stock, Pablo's eyes danced with excitement. He diffidently held out his hands.

I pulled back the bolt and made sure the chamber was unloaded. Then I took the leather caps from the Bausch and Lomb variable power scope and handed to the trembling youth the sweetest rifle ever made.

He took it reverently and tried it to his shoulder. He looked through the telescopic sight and fixed the cross-hair reticle on a distant rock and squeezed the trigger. There was the click of the falling firing pin. Pablo sighed. "Eef that had been a deer, we would have had venison steaks for dinner."

"Right now I would settle for some pancakes," I said, and took the rifle from him, firmly. He gazed wistfully at the beautiful Winchester as I slipped it back into the case; then, with a mighty sigh, he handed me a tin plate heaped with pancakes.

"That ees the most beautiful gun what I ever deed see." He was unusually silent during breakfast. I told him of my many adventures with that rifle, of a moose hunt in Canada, half a dozen deer hunts in New Mexico, a jaunt into old Mexico after the fierce little peccary, or *javelina*, which could tear a man to shreds if he missed his first shot. Pablo listened dreamily.

"There ees somet'ings wonderful about a beautiful gun," he almost whispered. "Eet ees true. Eet weel always shoot where eet ees supposed to. Eet weel always stand by you. Eet weel never let you down. Eet contains the heart of a man because some man who could make fine t'ings made eet weeth hees own hands, working long and hard to make eet strong and true and *muy, muy hermosa.*"

I was astonished. Pablo was putting into his halting words the admiration which every outdoorsman has for a fine gun.

"Pablo," I said, seeking to change the subject, "I think we'll go back to the hogan and see if the rug is done. I'll wash the dishes if you will catch those two rambunctious ponies."

"Si, *señor.*"

By the time the dishes were washed, Pablo was back with the two horses. As we engaged ourselves with the task of cinching up the saddles, I said, "Pablo, have you any idea how I may be able to get that rug? They don't seem to want to sell it."

"That gun, you would not sell eet?"

"Forget the gun for a moment, Pablo. You know Indians better than I do. How can I get that rug?"

"Do you want to sell those gun?"

"Of course not," I said impatiently. "It cost a lot of money. Besides, it means a lot to me. I have no intention of selling it, even if you offered me twice what it cost—and that is $200. That gun means more to me than money."

"And the Bi-mah Begay rug, she means more than money," said my Mexican friend quietly.

Pablo and I had been working back to back. I gave the cinch a last tug and whirled around to look deep into the serious eyes of my friend.

"You weel not sell the gun. She weel not sell the rug. Why do you not geeve the gun for the rug?"

I snorted. "And just what would grandma do with a Model 70 with a Bausch and Lomb scope? Hang a loom from it?"

"Bi-mah Begay she has a son, *que no*? He ees name

Diego, *que no?* She loves heem, *que no?* That son she ees a Navajo. A Navajo she weel almost sell the soul for a nice gun."

I looked at him for a long moment and picked up the gun case, tying it securely to the saddle strings.

It was late in the afternoon when we passed Battle-ship Rock on our way to the little plateau of Mother Begay's dwelling place. As our horses nosed over the ridge, we saw her sitting there exactly as before. She seemed not to have moved. A sleepy horse, badly in need of a currycomb, was ground-anchored before the hogan. Diego was coiling a rope.

"*Halah' hodzah!*" I called cheerfully.

"Howdy," came the laconic answer.

Bi-mah Begay turned her head slightly toward us and continued with her work. I saw to my delight that the rug was almost finished. She was working entirely with white now. I dismounted, and while Pablo struck up conversation with Diego, I moved over toward the old weaver.

"How beautiful!" I cried, as my eyes drank in the matchless coloring of the rug. The old woman smiled, but did not answer. I moved over to Diego.

"The rug is almost finished, isn't it?"

"Almost."

"Have you thought it all over? Will you sell the rug to me?"

"We do not care to sell the rug. I know that science must be served," he shrugged, "but we will not sell the rug," he repeated.

Pablo shot me a warning glance. As though he were asking for the time of day, he said, "Do you ever do any hunting?"

"This is an Indian reservation," came the stiff answer. "No one else is allowed to hunt."

"We know that. But I jus' was ask you, Do *you* ever hunt?"

"Once in a while. There are a lot of antelope near here. They are hard to hit, though. They run too fast. Have to shoot thirty feet ahead of one a hundred yards away running at right angles. I am pretty good at it, though," he said, proudly.

"*Mi amigo,* she has one fine gun," said Pablo innocently. "Can I show thees Diego those rifle weeth the glass sights?"

"Certainly," I said with a lump in my throat.

Pablo went to the palomino and untied the carved scabbard. Imitating me, he stood before the tall Navajo youth and dramatically drew the beautiful rifle from its case. He twisted the caps from the scope sight and placed the hunting piece in the hands of the Indian. That lanky individual lost no time in throwing the rifle butt against his shoulder. As Pablo had done before him, he picked out a distant rock and aimed at it.

"Gimme a cartridge," he demanded.

Silently I handed over the long brass cylinder and watched the Indian youth expertly flip it into the chamber. His eyes swept the skies. There was a shrill "Creeee!" of a high-circling hawk. Diego swung the rifle upward for an impossible shot. There was a mighty blast which echoed from hill to hill. To my amazement the hawk crumpled in mid-air and fell like a stone. I watched it hit the ground in a shower of feathers three hundred yards away.

I glanced over at Mother Begay. She was still weaving at the loom. She had not dropped a stitch.

Diego was breathing rapidly. He was looking at the rifle in his hands with the adoration most men reserve for a lovely woman.

I glanced back at Bi-mah Begay. She was slowly unrolling the rug. It was finished. I stood rooted to the spot with wonder.

"Diego," I caught my breath and plunged, "your mother thinks too much of the rug to sell it. It is the product of her skilful hands and her loving heart. I can understand that now. And you are holding something which I would not sell. It has become a part of me in many trips into the wilderness. I think more of that piece of steel and wood than I do of any lifeless thing on the earth. I would not sell it to you, but," I found it hard to say the words, "I will give it to you if you will cause your mother to give me that rug."

Something in the simple way I said the words

touched the heart of the Indian. He looked long and questioningly into my eyes.

"What will you do with the rug?" he asked. "Will you give it to some eastern scientists to dissect and take apart while they search for some anthropological curiosity? Will it be hung up somewhere to gather dust in a museum?"

"No, Diego. No one will ever get the rug away from me to keep. I shall let the men of science have it for a few months of study, but then I shall take it back and own it forever. You see, that rug means everything to me now. It is the symbol of life—the way I want to live it."

While we had been engaged with the rifle, Bi-mah Begay had finished the rug and was rapidly binding its edges. The Indian youth went over to his mother and talked with her earnestly for a few moments. I anxiously watched her wrinkled face.

Diego motioned to me, and I went over to the old weaver. She looked long at me. Again my soul was bared before her washed-out old eyes as she probed my heart. Finally satisfied with what she saw, she suddenly thrust the rug into my hands.

As we swung our mounts about with their heads toward the sunset, I had a fleeting, heartbreaking glimpse of a tall Indian youth stooping to enter a mud-daubed hogan. From under his arm protruded a gun case carved by old Sam Myers of El Paso.

Today as I write these words, Bi-mah Begay's masterpiece hangs on the wall of my study. It casts its mystic spell over me every time I enter the room. Bi-mah Begay has been gathered to her fathers, and as my eyes rest upon the beautiful work of her hands, I am reminded that the shadows are lengthening over the loom of my own life. God may be standing with his scissors in his hand. That does not matter; it is none of my business. My work is just to keep on weaving, a little here, a little there.

Now and then as I look at the rug, it seems to fade away and in its place I see a wind-swept desert plateau with the purple hills in the hazy distance and lazy sheep curled in the shade of old Battleship Rock. I again see a mud-plastered hogan facing toward the point where the sun will rise tomorrow with its hope of a brighter day upon the earth, and I see the old Navajo weaver, her faded old eyes looking clear to the throne of God while her heart and mind and hands move across the loom of time in tune with the Great Spirit.

Peace, ineffable peace, sweet and abiding, settles over my soul, and I can lay my weary head upon the bosom of God.

THE END